MW00532261

The
BEACH HOUSE

Brenda Mize Garza

The BEACH HOUSE

Brenda Mize Garza

Copyright © 2018 Brenda Mize Garza.
Illustration of Meet the Gang by Myca Nutt.
The seahorse, starfish and sand dollar illustrations are by Juan Mora.

All rights reserved. No part of this book may be used or reproduced by
any means, graphic, electronic, or mechanical, including photocopying,
recording, taping or by any information storage retrieval system
without the written permission of the author except in the case of
brief quotations embodied in critical articles and reviews.

LifeRich Publishing is a registered trademark of
The Reader's Digest Association, Inc.

LifeRich Publishing books may be ordered through booksellers or by contacting:

LifeRich Publishing
1663 Liberty Drive
Bloomington, IN 47403
www.liferichpublishing.com
1 (888) 238-8637

Because of the dynamic nature of the Internet, any web addresses or
links contained in this book may have changed since publication and
may no longer be valid. The views expressed in this work are solely those
of the author and do not necessarily reflect the views of the publisher,
and the publisher hereby disclaims any responsibility for them.

Any people depicted in stock imagery provided by Getty Images are
models, and such images are being used for illustrative purposes only.
Certain stock imagery © Getty Images.

KJV: Scripture taken from the King James Version of the Bible.

ISBN: 978-1-4897-1595-1 (sc)
ISBN: 978-1-4897-1594-4 (hc)
ISBN: 978-1-4897-1593-7 (e)

Library of Congress Control Number: 2018904006

Print information available on the last page.

LifeRich Publishing rev. date: 08/29/2018

This book is lovingly dedicated to my husband, Jesse, my daughters, Angela and Amanda, my son, Brian, and especially my grandchildren. Without them, this book would have remained silent.

Commit thy works unto the Lord and thy thoughts shall be established.

—Proverbs 16:3

CONTENTS

CHAPTER I
The Beginning

Where do you start when you have so much to tell? It's hard to know when and where it all began. Just yesterday, we were all carefree and playing in the ocean with our friends, collecting seashells, and making sandcastles. Sometimes when I stop and think about all the things we've seen and done, it's like a dream or a movie you may have seen as a child and looking back on those memories as if they really had taken place in your very own life.

Let me start by introducing myself, I'm Andrew. Hi, it's nice to meet you. I'll start from when we first saw them and fill in the rest as the story unfolds. Some of you will think this is a child's imagination gone wild, others will be afraid, and some may just put this book down. Whoever you are, please believe me, this is all real.

The sky was bright blue with just a hint of soft, whispering white clouds scattered across it. Some looked like animals at play while others looked just like plain old clouds. The sun was bright and hot, but we hardly noticed. The cool breeze came in across the water, giving us a little touch of ocean spray. *The ocean always looks so appealing to me*, I thought as I joined my friends. It seemed to hold untold stories of all those who had traveled on it, played in it, or just gazed at it as I was doing then. I turned my attention to my friends and away from the magnificent view, which always captivated me.

Everyone was there playing at the beach as we always did—our usual gang. At least that's what the boys called us. Of course, the only girl in our group of adventurers, Paige, wouldn't agree to that name. According to her, we were all just good friends and would be forever.

Allen and Lee were building a sandcastle with a large moat of course. They always put incredible detail into their walls and towers. Lee gathered ocean water in buckets to fill the moat never caring that most if not all the water sank into the sand. Allen was busy running in what seemed like all directions gathering seashells to add to the tower walls and to make windows. Such hard work, and so sad that by the next morning this project of love would end up mostly back where it had come from—the ocean. But that thought never seemed to deter the two of them from building the great sandcastle, as they liked to call it.

Paige was resting on her beach towel listening to music and reading a romance novel. I put my towel on a level spot close to her trying not to make the sand fly. Paige had a thing about making the sand fly. It got on her skin, which she drenched with suntan lotion, and that just wouldn't do. She'd storm back into the water, wash the mess off, and start all over. You know how girls are.

"What's Michael spouting off about?" I asked as I slowly lowered myself onto my towel thinking, *don't make the sand fly, don't make the sand fly,* with a little chuckle under my breath.

"You know," Paige said peering at me over her large Hollywood sunglasses, "Michael is playing his usual pirate game. Today, he's washed up on this deserted island. A fierce storm ripped his ship apart, and he fears he's lost most if not all of his crew."

She did a great imitation of Michael—even his hand gestures and cocking of one eye. It made me laugh so much that I thought my side would burst. Paige had a little grin on her suntanned face as she went back to reading.

Using his spyglass, Michael appeared to be checking out the lay of the land and talking loudly as if on stage. As usual, we were his audience. "Searching for me lost mates or maybe the local tribe," he said. "Will the tribes be friendly or man-eaters? One never knows what one might find when the ocean decides she no longer wants you riding her waves and tosses you to and fro until your ship is ripped apart, leaving you drifting for days on a wooden plank and baking in the hot sun. Suddenly, without warning, she finally spits you out onto the sand of her mighty shores!" He continued speaking loudly of the great unknowns he was about to face.

"Hey Michael, watch it," I shouted trying to keep him from falling over me, but I was a second too late. Tumbling over me, Michael headed face-first toward the great sandcastle. That sent Lee and Allen into a massive scramble to protect it and to get out of Michael's way. However, they weren't fast enough to keep from tangling up with him. Apparently, this was of great amusement to Paige. She rolled in the sand with laughter. The lotion she just applied was now mixed with brilliant white sand.

We all began laughing at how Michael, with one step, created this domino effect, causing all of us to end up on top of what was once the great sandcastle. We all ran into the ocean, splashing each other and riding the waves. Well, except for Paige. She was still trying to get the lotion and sand mixture off her skin. That was a real sight to behold. Have you ever watched someone try to get lotion and sand off his or her skin? Kind of reminds me of a dog chasing his tail and knowing he'll never catch it.

Suddenly, we were all facing the beach house standing in the water with the waves lapping against us. With each passing wave, we swayed back and forth trying not to fall. We were lined up side by side as if waiting for someone to take roll call. We stood there in such a way that you might say we were being drawn in the direction of the beach house. Just standing, looking, and waiting on someone to look back at us.

The beach house was extremely close to the water's edge. It had been there as long as we could remember. I'd never really thought much about it until then. It was strange how the tide came in and out all along the beach but never came near the beach house. It is as though the water knew what we would soon learn.

Of course, we dared each other on many occasions to

go into the house. We were kids, and kids love to dare each other—like the time Allen dared Lee to go into the caves looking for bats. Lee looked as if he had seen a ghost when he came running out of the cave as though his feet were on fire. Following right behind him were what seemed like a million bats darting out in all directions. That caused all of us to take cover under our beach towels hoping the bats would miss us. We called him batboy for a while. That is, until Paige convinced us to stop. "You're going to give him a complex if you keep that up," she told us in the most adult voice she could muster.

Standing in the waves, we continued to stare at the beach house. The silence was broken by Michael's declaration of a new, and exciting adventure.

"Today, I have decided," Michael began, which broke the trace that had held us captive. "I shall lead us into the beach house!" Tilting his head back, hands on his hips, chin pointed slightly up, he looked as if he were trying to appear taller than he was.

"That's right," he said. "I'll lead us into that old house, and you'll see once and for all that there's nothing strange about it. It's just an old house on the beach that was probably owned by an old couple in their forties. When they died, there was no one to leave the house to," he said as if he had inside knowledge.

Michael was the bravest one in our little merry band; he was afraid of nothing and no one. We had seen him with our own eyes face an angry dog, he starred at the dog until it just laid down. Old Mr. Mitchell's house was where the dog lived, and he protected the house when Mr. Mitchell was away on business. It seemed like he was always away on business. When our soccer ball landed right in the middle of his backyard, Paige yelled at Michael as he disappeared over the fence. Of course, Michael heard her but as usual didn't pay any attention. We rushed up and over the fence to help Michael or else to see our friend's fate; we were sure he would be in the jaws of Duke, the dog. Much to our surprise, Michael was facing Duke, starring right into the big dog's face. Duke seemed to melt. He laid down right in front of Michael, wagging his tail as if they had been friends forever. That was how it was with Michael. He was our hero that day. No one had gotten bit, and the ball remained in one piece. But the best part was that Duke became a member of our soccer team. He played on Michael's team of course.

It was lunchtime, so the beach house would have to wait until we all had our fill of tasty sandwiches, cookies, and lemonade. "We can't go on this mission without grub in our stomachs," Michael shouted as he challenged his younger brother to race him home. So off we went to see what our moms had waiting for us.

Michael and Allen raced toward their home, Michael of course was not running at full speed to allow his younger brother to win. He always liked to hear Allen say, "Roll Tide, Roll! I win!" Then Allen would let out a laugh we could hear all the way to our house.

CHAPTER 2
Them

With our bellies full of grub, we could now proceed with our mission. The sun was starting to hide behind the cliffs at Bay Point. The tide was gently going out further and further from the beach leaving behind seashells washed in by its waves. The shells were shining as the waves swirled white sand around them. With each wave, it appeared to be telling the shells goodbye with a whimsical laugh.

You know, no one goes into the creepy old house until it is almost dark. What kind of adventurers would we have been if we'd gone into the house in broad daylight?

We walked toward the old beach house. Lee was right behind Michael. Though Lee was younger than Michael, he always wanted everyone to know that Michael was not the only brave one in our gang. However, we all know it was Michael who never backed down.

Allen was right on the heels of Lee. Paige and I brought up the rear.

Most of the houses at Shell Cove looked like typical houses built around the ocean. They had bright colors and were trimmed mostly in white, and their large porches faced the ocean. The old beach house, however, was like none of the other houses. We called it the beach house because it was on the beach, not that it looked like a beach house. It stood out because it was so different. It reminded me of houses we read about in our history class; it was a house that you might have found on a large southern plantation. The roof was pointed in many areas, gables I believe they were called. The paint was long gone. Most of the wood was bare. The house had a large porch that wrapped around it. When looking at the porch it reminded me of a moat around a castle, a form of protection from the outside world.

On the front porch was a beautiful old swing. The swing could be seen swaying back and forth with the wind. We all wanted to try it out. If Michael had his way, we'd be swinging on it sooner than later.

Approaching the house, we were singing, laughing, and joking around as friends did when they were about to face danger and maybe even certain death. For what lay ahead of us, we could not have imaged, even though most children, as you are aware, have pretty active imaginations. We were no exception especially when we were at our special place in the caves. There, our imaginations were filled with grandiose thoughts and plans on just how to take these from thoughts to reality.

As we approached the house, a little smile appeared

across the old wooden planks that were in need of a fresh coat of paint. The porch seemed to be inviting us to come on in.

We ran up the large wide steps onto the porch and found ourselves right in front of an enormous door. That's when we all seemed to stop at the same time. I believed I've heard my mom call it a "screeching halt."

Paige later talked about how pretty the details in the carvings around the windows and the large door were. But at that moment, all we could see was the door. Michael began opening the door—slowly at first. Then as if he had received a new burst of courage, he flung the door wide open almost pulling it off its hinges. That startled us half to death!

Paige saw them first, but she didn't say a word. She just stared at them with her mouth wide open. Pointing in their direction. We stopped in our tracks, as if we were joined together, and moved in synch, one with the other. That's when even the bravest of the brave ran as if his life was in danger, and maybe it was! There was nothing else we could do, except to follow Michael as fast as we could run until we could run no more. We ended up out of breath and fell one by one onto the whitest sand in the world. We felt safe at that area of the beach. We were back where we belonged—on our little piece of paradise.

After that, no one spoke of what we had seen that day or even mentioned, the house on the beach. We continued to play in the ocean, collect seashells, and build sandcastles. As if nothing had ever happened. As if we had never gone inside that old house on the beach.

But, we had gone into that house. We had seen what was in that house, however, we never spoke of it, until today. This day turned out to be just another day. At least that is what we thought.

Then, they showed up.

CHAPTER 3
The Rescue

We were playing on the beach when we noticed a stranger on our little piece of paradise. We later learned that his name was Mr. Waters. A very unusual name especially since he was extremely interested in the spooky house on the beach, the one no one would go near—you know, because it had some things inside that we at Shell Cove didn't like to speak about.

Mr. Waters and Ms. Sue, our local realtor, were about to enter the house. We watched and waited to see it they—you know, the ones in the house—would make themselves known to Mr. Waters and Ms. Sue.

Michael said, "We have to go near the house just in case they need our help."

So off we went to protect the adults. It was amazing to me that we thought we could protect the adults. How soon we had forgotten that not long ago, we ran out of that house as fast as we could. We had never spoken about that day in

the house and certainly hadn't gone there again until now. Approaching slowly, we kept out of sight of Ms. Sue and Mr. Waters, but we got close enough to see inside. So, you know what that means, we are at the windows peering in with eyes wide open. We were waiting, even excited, to see them again.

"Mr. Waters, come on in," Ms. Sue said as she opened the door.

As they went inside, Ms. Sue was telling him of the house's many great features. She warned him that the house sat closer to the water than is currently allowed. "However, this house has never flooded," Ms. Sue said as if the thought had just occurred to her.

Mr. Waters didn't seem to hear anything Ms. Sue was saying. He appeared to be in another place and maybe another time, yet still physically there with her.

Then it happened. Only that time, the house began to fill with furniture. When Mr. Waters and Ms. Sue entered the rooms, they would come to life. The rooms were just as they had been when the previous owners lived there. Music was playing softly in the background. *Music?* I wondered. Mr. Waters appeared to be very comfortable and not afraid. His face shined with anticipation as if the place was exactly what he had hoped for.

Ms. Sue, however, continued to show the house to Mr. Waters as if nothing was happening. As if it were a normal house. Yet we knew there was nothing normal about this house. It was coming to life, but Ms. Sue seemed totally unaware of that.

Allen broke the silence. "Look! Ms. Sue acts as if she can't see the furniture appearing right before her eyes! Is she deaf too? The music is very beautiful, but she seems not to notice anything unusual."

"*Shh!*" Lee said as quietly as possible. "We don't want them to know we're here!"

"Sorry," Allen said in a whisper.

"Why can't Ms. Sue see them?" Paige asked. Then continued without giving anyone a chance to answer. Not that any of us had an answer. "Can they let some people know they're here and keep others totally unaware of them?"

Suddenly, a shape appeared, but it wasn't clear enough to see. It was like something you saw in the water and couldn't make out completely. It reminded me of the day we were snorkeling for hidden treasure at the cove. Paige had been sure she'd seen a large diamond at the rocky edge of a cave, so off we went to retrieve our newfound riches. Lee and Allen were already making big plans. "We'll all buy a large ship, one we can live on, and we'll go treasure hunting every day. We'll have a crew of course to sail the ship while we search maps looking for lost treasures."

Sorry. Sometimes I do that. I didn't mean to leave you hanging.

The shape was moving toward Mr. Waters. It slowly turned into a young lady about twenty or so. She went right up to Mr. Waters as if she knew him. She appeared unafraid to reveal herself to him. She was holding a beautiful scarf. The colors were bright, and it shined as if millions of little diamonds and other jewels had been sewn into the fabric. She handed the scarf to Mr. Waters. I saw three objects attached to the scarf. They dangled as she extended it to him. The objects were—a sea horse, a starfish, and a sand dollar.

Mr. Waters took the scarf without hesitation, and they exchanged words. We pressed our ears against the windowpanes trying to hear what the lady was saying. That of course blew our cover. Have you ever tried to be quiet while trying to listen to a conversation you weren't supposed to hear? The noise seemed to startle the young lady and she disappeared. Mr. Waters turned quickly in our direction. Being kids, we were long gone. The only proof of our being there were our face and handprints on the old windowpanes.

CHAPTER 4
The Plan

"*D*id you see the beautiful furniture?" Paige asked. "I bet its hundreds of years old." Paige's granddad was an antiques dealer, and he had taken Paige to many antique shows she would talk about for weeks. You know how girls are; they can go on and on about nothing. Paige probably even knew what style of furniture was in that house.

"Who cares about that old furniture?" Michael asked as he gasp and tried to catch his breath. "And what was that scarf all about? I wonder if the sea horse, starfish, and sand dollar have some secret meaning." He continued talking between taking a breath of air.

"You do realize that the old furniture, as you called it, appeared out of thin air, don't you?" Paige asked with hands on hips as if to emphasize her statement. The rest of us listened as Michael and Paige exchanged words.

The house and those who lived in it, was now the center of our world. Playing carefree on the beach had turned into spying on the beach house. We planned our next trip into the beach house—when we would go and who would be on lookout—but we all knew who would be point, Michael.

Paige agreed to talk with her granddad and get information on the furniture. "This will help us on our research prior to going back to the house," she stated emphatically. Paige liked to use big words such as *research*. Her mom was the brains in her family, and Paige knew she would follow in her mother's footsteps. One day, she too would have a PhD in something. Her granddad was very smart as well. He loved old furniture more than books unless the books were about old furniture.

Allen and Lee would spend time at the library looking through all the books about the houses in Shell Cove. They would ask Ms. Martha, the librarian, as many questions as they could think of concerning the beach house and those who once lived there.

Ms. Martha fancied herself as an authoritarian about all the old houses near or on the beach. She has dedicated her life to making sure all the old houses would never be destroyed. She was probably the reason the old beach house had never been torn down.

Lee said, "Allen and I will be on a reconnaissance mission until further notice."

That left Michael and me to go on an early mission. "Just to scope things out" is how Michael put it.

"Here's the plan," Michael said. "Tomorrow, we'll get up like normal because we don't want to give our parents anything to worry about. If they know we have plans to go into the old beach house, we'd be grounded for life, or longer! Once at our place on the beach, we'll take out our gear and get ready for the mission."

Michael's dad had been a marine gunny sergeant. His uniforms were so cool, and he had a chest full of medals. He got to shoot guns and drive tanks. Now, his dad wore suits and worked for NCIS. Michael liked to talk like him, and he planned to be a marine when he grew up. Go figure.

CHAPTER 5
The Mission

*J*ust as Michael and I geared up and headed to the beach house, fog began to roll in; it was thicker than we had ever seen.

"This won't stop the mission," Michael said with authority.

Listening to him talk was like listening to a smaller version of his dad. "We need to check our equipment before going any farther," Michael stated.

"What equipment are you talking about?" I asked.

"The walkie-talkies," he said as he pulled two green ones from his backpack.

"Nice!"

Walking to the house would be very tricky in the dense fog. So not to get separated, we tied a rope to each other's belt since holding hands would be out of the question. You don't hold hands on a mission.

Besides, we had our walkie-talkies. We checked them before heading to the beach house.

"Andrew, this is Michael. Can you hear me? Over."

"Yes, this is Andrew. I hear you loud and clear. Over and out."

The closer we got to the beach house, the better we could see it. The fog seemed to thin out around the house. Or was it the lights coming from the house that made it easier for us to see it? Lights! There was no electricity connected to the house, and there was no generator—nothing that would allow lights to be on.

We turned our flashlights off, we stood in awe as we watched the activity going on inside the house. The first day we saw them, there were only three. Now the house appeared to be full of shadows. We were too far from the house to make out anything for sure.

As we approached the house, crawling slowing on our hands and knees, Michael said, "This is how we approach the enemy, as if we're marines on a mission."

Sometimes, being the oldest of the gang was hard. It was nice being part of our adventurous group of kids. But I knew that I'd soon no longer be a part of this. It was sad to think about growing up and leaving my childhood friends. Because I was the oldest, I'd be the first to leave this beautiful island. When we were doing things like Michael and I were, it was hard to believe any of us would ever leave this island. You see, we live here all the time. Most of the other people on the island came and went with the season. Jackson was the only other guy my age there all the time, but he wouldn't be caught dead with our gang. "Too childish" was I believed, how he put it. Jackson had bigger plans than fooling around with us.

Just as we were creeping up to the windows to look at what was happening inside, the lights went out and all went absolutely silent. You know, like when it's so quiet you can hear a pin drop.

The fog began to get thicker and thicker. We couldn't see two feet in front of us, but I was sure we'd be okay because of the rope that connected us and particularly our walkie-talkies. Just moments after this thought had arrived in my brain, it was quickly found to be untrue. The walkie-talkies had worked well until the fog rolled in.

"Michael, can you hear me? This is Andrew. Over." The Walkie-talkie was silent. "Michael, come in if you can hear me!" The silence was so loud and yet so quiet. I know that doesn't make sense, but you get the picture.

Pulling on the rope that was tied to Michael made the fear in me rise. The rope went slack. I pulled it faster, and faster, closer and closer came the rope, but Michael wasn't on the other end. "Michael! Where are you?" My voice began to tremble, and my heart began to race. My heart was beating so loud, I could hear it pounding out the thoughts of my fear, with each and every beat. Terror was now gripping me so tight that I could hardly breath. Frozen in place and afraid to move. I began calling softly for Michael again, hoping he would be the one to answer. "Michael, please don't do anything stupid," I said under my breath. He was known to charge, after all, one day he would be a soldier. And charging is what they do.

Memories began to flood my thoughts, like the day we were only going to see what the new kids were doing. Watch from a distance. The next thing we knew, Michael was right there in the middle of them telling them his rules they'd have to follow if they wanted to be on our beach. The biggest kid in the group went right up to Michael and stood toe to toe with him, but Michael never flinched. He just cocked his head to one side and spat on the ground. The big kid moved his foot just in time not to receive what Michael had just let loose.

That day, Paige said, "We have to help Michael." So off we went to back up our fearless leader. When the new kids saw us running toward them, they ran away as fast as they could. We of course thought it was us they were running from. Later, we would learn it was them, they had seen.

I shook off my thoughts and got back to the task at hand—finding Michael. *Have they seen us? Is this why the house went dark and the music stopped? Or was there something else going on we couldn't see? And where's Michael?*

Suddenly, the lights and music came on. I turned quickly in the direction of the house. I couldn't believe my eyes. That's right, Michael was right in the middle of them talking of course as if he'd known them forever. *What to do? Do I go into the house or run for help? Help? What am I thinking? This is a secret mission. I can't run for help, and who would believe me anyway?*

I stared in disbelief of what was happening right before my eyes. However, I couldn't help but notice that the people Michael was talking to; they appeared to be normal. One of the three men I saw appeared to be a few years older than the others. They were dressed in blue jeans, button-down shirts, and boots. Nothing strange or out of the ordinary except maybe the boots; after all, it was a beach house. The women—or I should say ladies; none of them appeared to be much older than twenty—were dressed in sundresses and sandals.

Michael was wide eyed and talking at full speed about us. "Andrew's the oldest and smartest. Lee talks about nothing but old buildings. Allen is all about seashells and horses. Paige is the only girl in our gang. She's not all bad as girls go. She can be as tough as any of us. That leaves me." Michael's shoulders went back, and his chest went out. "I'll be a marine one day just like my dad."

The group seemed to be all ears as they listened to Michael. Suddenly, Michael clammed up. I thought he must have realized whom he was talking to. He turned pale and sweat began twinkling slowly down both sides of his face. The pretty lady we had seen earlier came from the back of the group. She looked friendly, and she was smiling. She put her hand out to Michael, and he extended his hand to her. And then they were all gone—just like that! Michael was sitting on a chair right before they disappeared. When they left, so did the chair. Michael was let down onto the floor like a feather you released from your fingers. Now he was sitting on the floor, all alone.

I ran into the house with my flashlight on bright. "Michael, what were you thinking coming in here by yourself? And what just happened? Where did they all go? And how about the furniture and the music? Michael, tell me—what were you thinking? Again, I asked as if he had not heard me the first time. You know nothing about these people if that's what they are. They look like people, but people don't disappear right in front of you, do they?"

Michael sat there as though he couldn't move. *Have they done something to him?* I wondered. *What if Michael isn't Michael anymore? What if he's now one of them?* "Stop it!" I said out loud, as if what I was thinking needed to be stopped with words spoken, not just silent thoughts that only I could hear. My outburst startled Michael. He quickly jumped to his feet, as if the floor beneath him became extremely hot.

"Did you see them, Andrew? Did you?" he asked me with a new-found urgency in his voice.

"Of course, I saw them just as I saw you right dab in the middle of them. How did you get in here? What were you thinking?" *Is that the third time I asked him that?*

"I have no idea how I got in here, Andrew!"

"Let's go, Michael. We need to meet up with the rest of the gang. Maybe the information they've gathered might help us make some sense of all this."

Michael was hesitant to leave. "Maybe they'll come

back now that you've joined me here." There was a sadness I could hear in his voice.

"Michael, I have a strange feeling that we're not the reason they left so quickly. Maybe they're not the only ones we can't see."

So, we headed for home. We no longer needed our flashlights; the fog was gone. I usually didn't walk Michael to his house after we left the beach, but today was different. I wanted to be sure Michael, made it home safely. That thought was very strange to me. I'd never thought about any of us not making it home safely until then.

CHAPTER 6
The Furniture

"**G**randdad? Are you here?" Paige asked as she walked into his antique shop.

"Paige, I'm in the back. I can't wait for you to see the new shipment of furniture that just came in!"

Paige paled as she saw the new— old—furniture her granddad was unloading.

"Where did this come from?" she asked.

"Remember my trip to England last month? I thought I'd lost the bid on this whole group, but today, it just showed up! I hope that dealer in England will return my call soon and clear up this mystery. What do you think, Paige?"

Without losing a moment of time, Paige began telling her granddad all about each and every piece. Her granddad beamed with joy at his granddaughter's appreciation for old furniture. Paige traced each line on the furniture looking at all the details that the craftsman had engraved into the corners of the chest of drawers. She

opened each drawer hoping to find an old letter or anything that would tell her about the owner.

"Granddad, who owned this furniture?" Paige asked trying not to sound excited.

"I'm not sure, but I could ask the dealer when he calls back. Why do you ask?"

"Just curious. It looks like the furniture I saw in some friends' house the other day."

"What friends? This is rare furniture, not what you'd normally see here in Shell Cove."

Oh, why did I say friends? she asked herself. *Granddad knows all my friends.* "Some new kids we met last week," Paige said hoping her granddad wouldn't notice the expression on her face as she told that little white lie. *Friends? I'm not sure what they are. Why would I call them friends?*

Just as Paige was ready to go, she caught a sound coming from one of the bedside stands. "Granddad, did you hear that?"

"What?" Glancing briefly in the direction of his granddaughter. He was busy inventorying all the furniture and gave little thought to what Paige had said.

Paige walked slowly in the direction of the noise she had heard. *What am I thinking? There's no noise.* Then she heard it again, only a little louder.

"Push the shell on the side of the drawer," the voice said.

Oh great. Now I'm hearing voices. She looked at her granddad and saw he was still busy checking off the items on his list. From the expression on his face, Paige thought he had not heard the voice coming from the nightstand. Paige did as the voice had directed her. She pushed the shell on the side of the drawer, and a hidden compartment appeared in the back of the nightstand. It was a small compartment, but she saw a piece of paper tucked neatly inside.

"Take it," the voice said.

That time, Paige didn't obey the voice. Instead she closed the compartment quietly, gave her granddad a kiss on his cheek, and left the shop.

She got home just as her mother was setting the table for dinner. "Can I help?" Paige asked her.

"Of course, you may, and thank you for being so helpful. Are you okay, Paige? You look a little pale."

"I'm okay, Mother. I just ran all the way from granddad's store, that's all."

Paige took the plates from her mother and continued to prepare the table for their meal.

When everyone was seated, Paige's granddad said a prayer to God thanking Him for their food and the many other blessings He had given them.

"Paige, why aren't you eating?" her mother asked.

Paige was stirring the food on her plate into little piles making sure nothing touched. About the time she had gotten all the vegetables where she wanted them, Allen kicked her under the table. That caused Paige to lose control of her fork, and all the peas she was moving around went flying across the room.

"Stop it!" she yelled at Allen, who was laughing uncontrollably. "You're going to pick them all up, Allen." She tried not to laugh at the peas scattered across the kitchen floor; they looked like tiny green marbles.

"What's wrong, Paige?" her mother asked again. "Why are you playing with your food? If you're not hungry, you may be excused. Take your plate to the sink."

That was great news to Paige. All she could think about was the hidden compartment. "Granddad, may I go into the store and look at the furniture again?"

"Of course, Paige. Just be sure to turn the alarm off when you go in and on when you leave."

"Okay, thanks!" She ran to put her plate in the sink.

Back at the store, Paige turned on the lights and turned off the alarm. The store was at the end of the block from her house—just a short walk—but of course she had run all the way there. She walked slowly toward the nightstand wondering if she would hear the voice again. She was doubting what she had heard earlier. However, before that thought could settle in her brain, she heard the voice again. She wasn't afraid of the voice, and she didn't even wonder where it was coming from. She went directly to the nightstand with the hidden compartment. She pushed the shell, and the compartment opened. She took the paper out, closed the compartment, and she headed for home. Back in her bedroom, she curled up in her favorite chair and read the letter.

If the compartment was open to you and you are reading this, it can only mean one thing - you, are the Reader. This message was hidden for you many years ago.

There are two worlds living on this island side by side. The worlds interact each day, but the humans normally do not know that the unseen world is even here.

There are two entities in this unseen world. One is friendly, and the other, let me just say, is not. Both entities in this unseen world can impact the seen world. However, they must be invited to do so.

This small island is the battleground between these two entities. The angels, as they are sometimes called, are on your side. By now, you have probably met some if not all of them. I know this because if you had met the others first, you would not have listened to my voice. Our Creator calls the angels you have met guardian angels. He has assigned them tasks. Each guardian angel has certain responsibilities.

The other entity, as you will soon come to know, are demons. They are here under the control and command of their master, who has been around for a very long time.

As the Reader, you will be given a task that is not to be taken lightly. Amethyst, one of the guardian angels, will soon introduce herself to you. Please listen carefully to what she has to say.

Paige slowly folded the letter back into its original shape and tucked it in her nightstand. She changed into pajamas and brushed her teeth. Just as she did every night, she kneeled beside her bed and prayed to God. Her prayer normally consisted of thanking God for His many blessings and asking Him to keep watch over her family and friends.

But that night, Paige added a new part to her prayer; she asked for wisdom and guidance to help her understand what the letter meant. She ran downstairs to give everyone a goodnight kiss and hug, and then she ran back upstairs to her room. She got into bed and turned off her lamp. She quickly fell into a peaceful sleep.

CHAPTER 7
Reconnaissance

*M*s. Martha, the librarian, was busy shelving books and mumbling under her breath about how lazy the younger generation was. "You'd think that when they realized they've taken the wrong book, they'd just put it back where it belonged." She was talking ever so softly; after all, it was a library. *Must not bother the readers*, she thought.

She was dressed in her normal attire—a blue skirt and a white blouse with a lace collar that lay neatly over the sweater she wore regardless of the temperature. She always looks professional; a beautiful colored haircomb kept her hair neatly in place.

"Ms. Martha, what can you tell us about the old beach house?" Lee asked trying to sound as if it were just a passing thought instead of what it really was—all he could think about.

Allen chimed in. "We're doing a research project on old houses here on Starfish Island. Everyone tells us you're the expert on these houses. They say it's your cup of tea. But I'm not sure what that means exactly. I don't like hot tea." He continued, as he walked away to pick up a book on horses he'd just spotted. His dad was a rancher and had many horses.

"That old house has been there as long as I can remember," Ms. Martha said. "To find the information, I'm afraid we'll need to go into the basement, boys." She walked to the back of the library until she came to a very large, old, wooden door.

"Strange. I've never seen that door before," Allen said," but I don't think I've ever been this far back in the library either."

Lee looked at the carvings on the door casing and thought, *I've seen those carvings before, but I can't remember where. Probably not important.*

"Be careful coming down the stairs," Ms. Martha said. "They can be a little tricky at times."

She stopped briefly outside the big door, switched on the lights. These lights were now illuminating the path down the narrow staircase.

"There may be a few cobwebs here and there," she said as she brushed one away. "No one really comes down here anymore," she said as if that thought had just occurred to her and needed to be spoken out loud.

Once they navigated the stairs, Ms. Martha turned on yet another a light. This new light seemed to make the basement and its contents come to life. Lee and Allen were amazed at what lay before them. They couldn't believe that there had been another world hidden beneath the library all that time. Their eyes darted in all directions trying to take it all in.

Ms. Martha was amused by the boys' expressions. She had forgotten how she had felt the first time she'd seen the hidden treasures under the library. The boys' reaction brought floods of long-forgotten memories rushing back. A smile of sheer pleasure could be seen on her face, and a slight, rosy blush covered her cheeks.

"Boys, take your time and look at everything, but please don't touch anything."

Lee and Allen began to take in each and every item. "Is this part of a ship?" Lee asked as he pointed to a wooden mermaid with raven hair and a beautiful scarf hung around her neck. The scarf had three objects at the end of it—a sea horse, a starfish, and a sand dollar.

"Why yes, Lee. That's from Captain Herbert Mize's ship. He named her the Lost Mermaid."

Allen was captured by the many sand dollars so neatly arranged in a glass case. "Someone must really like sand dollars to go to all this trouble of arranging them by sizes," he said.

Ms. Martha was standing in front of a large stack of old Bibles and carefully reading the notes attached to them until she found one in particular. She blew at the dust that was piled so thick on the covers of the bibles, it hardly moved, so she bushed it off with her hand. "Ahh, here it is." She took the old, black, worn Bible. She told the boys about how its owners had loved it and had read it over and over again. She turned the pages ever so gently for fear they might tear. She moved her fingers along each and every line of faded writing on one page until she got to the names at the bottom.

Ms. Martha said, "The owners were a couple that settled here on Starfish Island. They were part of the original families that established Shell Cove. The deed indicates that Steve and Judy Heinrich, a couple from Reading, England, were the original owners.

"Back in those days, people didn't go to the courthouse to write out their deeds. Everything that was important was recorded in their Bibles, things like marriages, births, and deaths. Those entries were considered legal documents." She explained to the boys.

"Not having any children of their own, Steve and Judy Heinrich left their house to the town of Shell Cove. The house can never be sold unless the entire town agrees to sell it. Well, that's not exactly true. Only the twelve main families who settled here have the right to sell the house. Any money will go to the town charter and to the upkeep of the lighthouse and anything the charter has listed. No one has ever wanted to buy the house." As if she were talking to just herself, she said, "Until last week. A Mr. Waters came in here asking all kinds of questions about that old beach house. Just like you two are doing right now."

Allen was still taking in all the seashells located in the old basement. But that last remark got his attention, he quickly moved in the direction of Ms. Martha. "Ms. Martha, what did you tell this Mr. Waters?" Allen asked as nonchalantly as he could—as if he really didn't care one way or the other. But he did care, we all cared.

"Strange. The old house has sat there for all these years.

No one seemed to care anything about it," Ms. Martha said as if having a conversation with herself or an unseen friend.

Lee and Allen thought they had gotten all of what Ms. Martha had to share. However, it was just the tip of a very large iceberg. Much more was hidden beneath the library. Just as they turned in the direction of the stairs, Lee noticed something that caught his attention and awakened his spirit.

"What's that, Ms. Martha?" Lee asked pointing in the direction of a mannequin of sorts. The mannequin was dressed in what appeared to be armour.

"That," Ms. Martha replied in an angelic tone, "is the armour of God." She chuckled to herself and then recanted a little. "What I should have said is that the armour on the mannequin represents the armour of God Paul talked about in Ephesians 6:11–17."

That new information had the boys' full attention. They stood still, waiting on Ms. Martha to elaborate further.

"Please, Ms. Martha, can you explain the armour to us?" Allen asked. The excitement in his voice was not only heard, it showed brightly on his face. How could she refuse?

"Let me get one of the Bibles and we'll go over this armour just as Paul described it."

She put two chairs in front of the mannequin and put the Bible on a table next to the mannequin to make it easy to read the verses and point to the pieces of armour. Allen and Lee eagerly sat down on the chairs that she had arranged for them.

"According to Paul," Ms. Martha began, "Put on the whole armour of God, that ye may be able to stand against the wiles of the devil."

Allen raised his hand as if he were in school and wanted to get the teachers attention.

"Yes, Allen?"

"Ms. Martha, what does wiles mean?"

"It's the trickery the devil uses to get people to do evil."

"Like when he wants me to talk bad about someone, right?"

"Exactly like that. Paul described each piece of armour and how it was to be used: 'Having your loins girt about with the truth.' Before you ask, Allen, loins refer to your lower back and waist," she said while pointing to that piece of the armour. That made the three of them burst out into a joyful laughter.

After the moment of laughter died down, she continued. "Having on the breastplate of righteousness; your feet shod with the preparation of the gospel of peace; above all taking the shield of faith, wherewith ye shall be able to quench all the fiery darts of the wicked, and take the helmet of salvation, and the sword of the Spirit, which is the word of God."

The two boys had even more questions concerning the armour. Ms. Martha looked at her watch and told the boys they would have to stop the lesson on the armour for today. She hadn't realized they had spent more than an hour in the basement. *What will the people in the library think about my being unavailable for such a long time? Surely, someone must have noticed I wasn't up there.* However, no one had missed her or even noticed she was gone.

Lee and Allen thanked Ms. Martha for her time and especially for taking them to the basement, which had been a total surprise for them.

Ms. Martha replied, "You're most welcome. Please let me know it you need anything else for your school project," she said as she led them upstairs.

As they near the top of the stairs, Allen turned to Lee and asked, "What school project?"

Lee quickly ushered Allen through the big door and out of the library. Lee's actions made Allen stop immediately once they were outside. "What do you think you're doing?" he asked Lee, with a look of concern on his face.

"The school project was our cover story, remember?" Lee said a little sterner than he meant too.

"Oh, yeah, that's right. You don't think I blew our cover, do you?" Allen asked, a little sheepish.

"No. I think Ms. Martha was too busy looking at the mess those teenagers left on one of the big tables."

The two boys talked about the many treasures they had seen in the basement. They had never believed that a boring trip to the library could turn out to be such a great adventure.

What Lee and Allen didn't see during their little interview of Ms. Martha was the many demonic spirits who were watching their every move. It was not as if the demons had just arrived on Starfish Island. They had been there for many of years causing unseen interference with the people who lived or visited the island. The demons really didn't care one way or the other about the humans who inhabited the little island; they caused them a little unpleasantness more out of boredom than anything else. What had gotten their attention was the beach house and its recent visitors. The visitors who had caught their attention were not Lee or Allen or the rest of the gang. It was them.

CHAPTER 8
The Debrief

"**W**hat were they like?" Paige asked.

"Were you scared, Michael?" Lee asked.

"I'm glad I wasn't there. I might have wet my pants!" Allen said.

"Where *were* you, Andrew?" they all shouted at once.

Before I could answer, Michael started off with his tale of the events.

"The fog rolled in thick, so thick we couldn't see our hands when we stretched them out in front of us." Michael standing in the middle of the gang, closed his eyes. He began stretching out his hands to demonstrate what he was telling them. "Andrew and I tied a rope to our belts, so we wouldn't get separated or worse—lost forever!"

That was Michael—never a dull story with him. You could ask him how his walk to school went, and he'd make it a great adventure.

Michael continued. "The fog cleared

as we got closer to the house. The lights were on. The people inside were gathered as if they were at a meeting or something"

"Lights?" they all asked excitedly. "What lights?"

Sounds like a rerun of Michael and I when we saw them, thought Andrew.

"Let me finish," Michael said all out of breath with excitement. "When I looked into one of the windows, a face appeared out of nowhere looking right back at me. Before I knew it, I was right in the middle of them. They all stared at me as if they knew who I was. Hmmm. Funny thing, though—none of them looked familiar," Michael said as if he had just remembered that. "I began sharing data about all of us with them."

Data. Just what a marine would say, I thought.

"When I was telling them all about us, I got this strange feeling that they already knew everything there was to know about each of us. Then, the lady we saw on our first trip to the house came up to shake my hand. Well, at least that's what I thought. She reached out her long, slender arm to me, so I put my hand right out to hers." Michael stretched his right arm out as far as he could. Demonstrating to the gang what he had done in response to the young lady's action.

"Before my hand could reach hers, one of the men looked at the lady. You know, like when your mom's about to do something and your dad doesn't think it's a good idea—that kind of look. And just like before, they were gone!" Michael said with a look of exasperation.

"Gone? What do you mean gone?" Lee asked.

"Just like before, they disappeared," Michael said with a sad expression on his face.

Our gang decided to go home, what else was there for us to do? They had disappeared, again.

"A good night's sleep is what we all need," Lee stated firmly. "Let's go home."

"Then we can get our thoughts together tomorrow on what will be our next plan of action," Michael said as we slowly left the beach.

Allen was bringing up the rear looking for more seashells. "You can never have too many," he said. "One day, you'll see. These will be very important items to have!"

We all laughed at the thought of seashells being important. But when we needed them, Allen had more than enough.

All the way home, the picture of Michael in the middle of them kept running through my brain. *Why had they let Michael in their midst? Who was the young lady who wanted to take Michael's hand? And who was the man who kept them from touching?* Every visit to the beach house gave us more questions than answers. *Maybe it's time to explore something or somewhere else. After all, school will start soon. We'll have little time for that old house.*

As soon as my head hit my pillow, I was out for the night.

The next thing I heard was mom's voice.

CHAPTER 9
Church

"Andrew, time to get up. Breakfast is almost ready, dear."

Mom's announcement made me jump out of bed, brush my teeth, and head downstairs. Before I could reach the first landing, my mom yelled, "Make sure Lee's up and getting ready."

Mom's yell was not really a yell. It was more like a loud whisper.

That's right, Lee is my younger brother. He didn't like for me to act as if we were related when we were with the gang. He was one of the reasons I was part of this gang. *Gotta keep an eye on him. He can always find something to get into.*

Not long ago, Lee thought he could get a better view of the cove if he climbed the highest tree in the park. That was a great plan. Until it came time for him to come down. He always did stuff before he thought stuff through. *Maybe it's because he's so young.*

"Hey, guys," Lee yelled from the top of the tree. "I can see the old lighthouse and all the ships in the harbor. I can even see Captain Earl George, the sea captain of the *Lost Ship*. Why would anyone name a ship that? Isn't it the captain's job to keep the ship from getting lost? Looks like he and his wife, Della, are getting ready to set sail."

Captain Earl and Della sailed for months at a time, "to wherever the winds want to take us," Captain Earl would say when ask where they were going. Della had a unique collection of jewelry she'd gotten in all the faraway places they'd traveled. She always brought our moms some jewelry when she returned from one of their special trips to some faraway lands.

"Come down out of that tree, Lee, or you're going to get us both in trouble," I yelled looking up at him.

"Well, all right," Lee shouted back. "I'm tired of looking around anyway." He started to come down from the limb he was sitting on when he did as most people that are afraid of heights do. That's right. He looked down. At that very moment, he froze like a statue. "Maybe I'll stay up here just a little longer. A ... A ... After all, I can see the whole wide world from here!"

"Don't make me have to come up there because if I do all of Starfish Island will know about this!" I yelled. "School will be starting soon. Your year will be long and painful if all the other kids in your class hear about how you were too scared to come down. That's right! Too scared!"

In the blink of an eye Lee was on the ground. I wasn't

sure how he'd done that. All I know is that he was suddenly standing beside me. But when I looked at him, his face was white as snow. His eyes as big as, well let me just say "wide eyes" cannot say enough. His only comment, "Just don't ask. You wouldn't believe me anyway," as if he knew what I was thinking.

That was Lee's first and last time to climb that tree. Anyway, back to that morning.

"Lee, get up," I shouted as I entered his room. "Mom said get up. Breakfast is almost ready."

Lee's room was filled with pictures of old buildings. "I'm going to restore them to their original design," he'd say. He loved old buildings. He could look at a building and picture it as it had been when it was new, the people who lived in it, and how the building was loved and cared for by the owners. "These old buildings have stories to tell," he'd say as he stared at them.

Lee would seem to get lost inside any building. I know that sounds weird, but I've watched him stare at them and be oblivious to anyone or anything around him. When I would ask him what he was doing, he'd say, "I was talking to the building of course!" Talking to the building. Like that was normal?

Breakfast was great as always. Mom was such a good cook, and she seemed to enjoy watching us eat. Every meal, she'd look at us as if she'd never seen us eat before. Mom was one of those moms whom all the kids in the neighborhood called mom. She'd always bring us lemonade and cookies when we gathered at our house to plan our next adventure. She was very active in the church and was always volunteering to help with functions at the school and the library. Yet she always had time for us.

I grabbed my backpack and headed out. "Mom, see you later!"

"Where do you think you're going, young man?" She asked.

"To the beach, Mom, to meet the gang," I said.

"Not today, Andrew. You know it's Sunday. We're going to church in an hour."

How could I forget it was Sunday? Especially since my dad was the pastor. Go figure.

Yep, our dad was the pastor. In fact, he was the only pastor there. Well, there were associate pastors at our church, but it was the only church in Shell Cove, the only town on Starfish Island. Shell Cove was small—population 700 during normal times. Normal times were when the tourists had gone home, and we had our island all to ourselves. The town council reminded everyone every year right before tourist season started, "The tourists keep our town alive!" As if the town died when they were gone. Our gang differed with the town council; it was when the tourists left that our little town came to life. That is what we would learn later from the beach house.

Church was normal. At least the sermon was. Dad told us about Jesus and that He had saved us from our sins—not just our old sins but even our future sins. That we must have faith in His finished work for us. There was no way for us to earn our way to heaven; it was a gift of God paid for by Jesus. Dad never seemed to grow tired of telling everyone how much God loves them and that God was the reason we were here. And that Jesus died for all of us.

Everyone knew that the pew next to the last one on the left side was reserved for us. Having a dad who was pastor had a few perks. We picked that one because the pastor's sons couldn't sit in the last pew; that would have been too weird. Dad liked to look more to his right when he was preaching, so we selected the left. That way, he wasn't always looking in our direction.

For such a small town, the church was always packed. The founding fathers of our little piece of paradise had God and church in all their legal documents. Maybe they knew that church would bring us all together like one big family. Don't get me wrong, not all the people in our town got along all the time, but somehow, we made all our differences work together.

"What's the plan?" Paige asked as the gang got seated on our pew.

Everyone turned to look at Michael, but he was preoccupied with his thoughts, at least that's how it appeared to us.

"Michael," Allen said a little too loud; several members of the congregation turned in our direction. You know the saying, "If looks could kill …"

"Michael," Allen whispered. "What's the matter? You deaf or what?"

Michael slowly turned in Allen's direction. His face was as pale as could be.

"Michael, what's going on?" Paige asked. "You look as if you've seen a ghost."

Just like that, Michael's face was back to normal. He replied, "Nothing. Why do you ask?"

We looked at each other and back to Michael, who seemed unaware of what had just happened. He said, "It's time we forget about that old beach house. We need to start focusing on school. Summer break will be over in a couple of weeks. Let's just spend time on the beach and in the surf while we can."

"I'm all for that," I said. "After all, water is my life!"

Paige couldn't believe her ears. *Give up on the beach house after all we've seen? I'm not going to let this go. I have that information on the furniture.* She was hoping that Allen and Lee had gotten more information from Ms. Martha. "We can't let this go now!" Paige said, with desperation in her voice. She saw that none of the gang was interested in what she had to say; their thoughts were only of the beach.

"Michael, don't get scared," the voice said.

Michael slowly turned in the direction of the voice. There was no one there. *Maybe I'm hallucinating*, he thought. But he heard the voice again, and a body appeared. He quickly looked at his friends; they were all engaged in conversation with each other unaware of what was happening right next to them.

"They cannot see or hear me," she said. "Try not to get excited! I just wanted to say hello and let you know I'm always available for you. Do you remember me from the beach house?"

"Of course, I remember you," Michael said with a big smile on his face. "It's so cool how you kept appearing and disappearing while I was talking to the rest of your friends. They are your friends, aren't they?" Michael asked for he was unsure about the relationships between the people at the beach house. "Why do I keep calling them people? No people I know can disappear." Michael said out loud, and was surprised to hear the words he was thinking actually coming out of his mouth. "What are you guys? We keep calling you people, but we all know that isn't true."

"First of all, you can call me Marti. And you're correct! We aren't people. We're heavenly spiritual beings. Everyone you have encountered so far is an angel. You may have heard us referred to as guardian angels. However, there are others that are here from time to time. They're not heavenly at all. They're demonic!"

With this new information Michael let out a loud "what are you talking about Marti?" This outburst even made the pastor stop talking. Now the whole congregation is starring at Michael.

Michael said, "I'm sorry, Pastor Judge. Please go on

with your sermon. It's very interesting." Everyone broke out into a loud laughter.

"That's okay," Pastor Judge said. "The sermon's over. I was just telling everyone I'll see them next Sunday."

Once the gang was outside the church, Michael was fired upon with question after question.

"Who's Marti?"

"Was he there with you?"

No one was allowing Michael to even get one word in.

"Stop!" Michael said, raising his hand in the direction of the gang. His voice just loud enough so it was heard above all the rest but not so loud as to attract the attention of the others leaving the church. "Marti is not a he, Marti is a she. She was at the beach house the night Andrew and I went on our mission," Michael began. "She never said anything to me until now. She just showed up right next to me on the pew! First, I only heard her talking. Then, she appeared just as they always do. She told me they were guardian angels, so we can start calling them what they really are. Guys, can we just drop this for now?"

He turned and walked quietly away from them. He didn't want to mention the part about the demons. That was too much for him, and he thought it would be too much for the others. He headed home. He appeared upset with this meeting he had just encountered in the church. No one went after him. He had made it clear he wanted some time alone.

"Hey Allen, Lee," Paige said. "Did you get any information from Ms. Martha about the beach house?"

"I thought we were supposed to forget about the beach house and start thinking about school," Allen replied.

"Michael is not the boss of us. We just let him think he's in charge because he likes that," Paige said. "So, what did you find out?"

"Apparently, Steve and Judy Heinrich built the old house when our town was founded," Lee said. "They must have been real big Christians because they wrote all kinds of information in their Bible. And the Bible looked really old and worn. Maybe they'd read it over and over just to make sure they understood what God was saying. You know, that's a very big book. Maybe that's how they died." He was thinking that the two of them must have carried the book everywhere they went. "You know, due to exhaustion from reading and carrying that heavy book."

"Lee!" Paige said firmly to shock him back into the present time. "People in those days had no way of keeping their information like we do today—in the courthouse or on computers. They wrote everything they felt was important in their Bibles. In fact, their Bibles were considered to be legal documents for family births and deaths."

"Paige, you're so smart. You know everything," Allen remarked.

"Well, not everything," she replied, "but quite a lot." She smiled with self-accomplishment. "But what else about the house?" she asked. *Trying to keep these two on track is like herding cats*, she thought, as a little grin appeared at the corner of her mouth. Her mom used that phrase to describe what it was like dealing with her students at the college where she taught.

"Apparently, the house belongs to the town now. That's why it's never been sold. No one's lived there since Steve and Judy Heinrich died," Allen added as if it was all he could remember right now. He and Lee both had forgotten all about the basement under the library and the armour of God Ms. Martha had told them about.

Everyone but Paige was thinking about the beach, building sandcastles, and collecting shells. After all, Michael had said it was time to have fun and forget about that old house. And we always followed Michael's advice. After all, he was the leader.

But Paige was persistent. "Where did they put all the furniture that once was in the house? Did she know what happened to it?" But her questions were to no avail. The boys ran off together. The only thing on their minds now, was having fun.

Back at the beach the gang had gathered, everyone except for Paige. They acted as if nothing strange had happened at church that morning. Michael, Allen, and Lee were building sandcastles individually. They planned to join the castles into one gigantic kingdom. I was swimming in the crystal-blue ocean enjoying each and every wave with a new appreciation. After all, school would start soon, and my time in the ocean would be limited.

"Hey! Look at the great shells that washed up last night!" Allen exclaimed. As he ran back to where Michael and Lee were building their castles. "These'll look great as doors," he said as he pushed the winged shells right in front of Michael's face.

"Really, Allen!" Michael yelled. "You just made me knock down my highest tower. Watch what you're doing!"

"Just trying to help," Allen said as he ran back for more shells. Not really caring about Michael's comment.

The sun was starting to slowly go down, shining brightly across the whitecaps. I joined Michael, Lee, and Allen on the beach.

"Where do you think Paige went?" I asked no one in particular.

"Probably to the library," Allen said not really caring one way or the other.

"That would do her no good. It's Sunday, and the library's closed," Michael said, evoking laughter from the others.

"I can see that look on her face right now," Lee said trying to make his face look like Paige's when she learned she'd been mistaken about something. And Paige was rarely wrong about anything.

"Let's head home, guys," I said.

Everyone started brushing the sand off their swimsuits and picking up their towels.

"Just one more quick dip in the water before we leave," I said.

We all ran into the surf, diving into the waves. The thought of going home for the night had been replaced with a thought of some last-minute fun.

CHAPTER 10
Paige's Adventure

*P*aige decided that if the gang would ever find out anything about the old beach house, she'd have to gather the information herself. That meant a trip to the library was her first order of business.

Thoughts were running rapidly through her head as she made her way through the narrow path to her destination. The pebble path she was on was making her wish she'd at least changed her shoes after church that day. She'd been in such a hurry when she parted ways with the rest of the gang that her attire had not been one of her priorities; getting to the bottom of the mystery of the beach house and its residents was.

Her tunnel vision didn't allow her to see the beauty of the woods and its many inhabitants. The birds were singing, the squirrels running and jumping from tree to tree, and the butterflies were dancing all around the flowers, but all that beauty was wasted on Paige. At least for the moment.

She could have taken the sidewalk down the main street, but that would have taken more time, and she wanted answers. Now. She wanted information that would explain the strange happenings at the old beach house, the furniture, and now the letter. *It seemed like an impossible task*, she thought. "But if anyone can get answers, I can," she said boldly with a smile of certainty.

As she neared the library, she realized it was Sunday. *I just left church! What was I thinking?* The thoughts of getting answers today had allowed her to forget the library was closed. *I'll have to wait until tomorrow. And so, will my questions.*

As she walked past the library, she was lost in thought about the old beach house, the furniture, the letter, and the people who kept appearing and disappearing. The next thing she knew, she was standing in front of the Star Café. Paige decided to go into the cafe', not knowing this would be a new adventure. And this time she would be the only one invited.

Paige's new adventure began at the little café on the corner of Sand Street and Ocean Boulevard. She opened the door as if she knew exactly what she would see inside, but she stopped in her tracks as though her shoes were nailed to the floor. *They're here*, she thought. She could sense their presence though she couldn't see them. *This is so strange. Why does it feel as if they're here? We've seen them only at the old beach house until this morning, when Michael saw one of them at church.* She quickly looked all around the room, glancing at each and every person in the café. Searching their eyes for any sign of the guardian angels.

"Paige, are you okay?" Mrs. Star asked as she walked up behind her.

"Why yes, Mrs. Star. Just looking for some friends."

Friends? What friends? Is that what I'm calling the guardian angels now? This is too bizarre, Paige thought as she searched the café for the right place to sit. She wanted to sit where she would have the best advantage to see the entire place. *What a joke!* She thought, and laughed softly. *Any seat will let you see the entire place!*

Paige made her way slowly across the little café to the empty corner booth. As she slid across the blue and silver seat, that strange feeling came over her again. Quickly she looked in all directions, seeming to spin her head around, she had to find the guardian angels. Oddly, the only one looking in her direction was Mrs. Star. *Does she sense their presence as well? Does she know something about the old beach house?* Nothing but more questions seemed to lay at every turn, no answers, only questions.

While Paige was scoping out the café, others—unseen by humans—were scoping out Paige. She had sensed a presence when she opened the door of this little café and thought it was the angels. It was not. It was another presence, and it was not friendly. The new presence wanted to keep Paige and the gang from completing their mission that lay ahead. A very important mission that would change their lives forever.

Mrs. Star walked over to where Paige sat, never taking her eyes off of her. "Paige," Mrs. Star said in her usual cheery voice. "What will you be having today, and where are the others? Without pausing to receive a reply she seemed to answer her own questions. Will they be joining you, or is this your day out?"

"Everyone went to the beach after church today. I was going to the library, but then I realized it wasn't open on Sundays."

"It's too early for school projects. Is there something you're researching? Maybe I can help," Mrs. Star said as if she knew something.

"I'll just have a soda and some fries," Paige replied acting as if she hadn't heard Mrs. Star's last few sentences. Turning toward the kitchen, Mrs. Star went to place Paige's order.

Johnny and Pam Star's ancestors were part of the original twelve families that settled on Starfish Island many years ago. Their ancestors were blacksmiths who came from England. When that trade was no longer needed on the island, they opened the island's first and only café.

"Paige." It was a voice so soft that Paige thought for a moment she was hearing things. "Paige." The voice was a little louder that time. She turned in the direction of the voice. Now sitting right across from her was a young lady. Thinking she was seeing and hearing things, Paige closed her eyes tightly, then opened them slowly. The lady just sat there, as if she was waiting on Paige to say something. Paige glanced around the room to see if anyone had noticed the lady seated across from her, which had just appeared. A couple seated at a table close to the door were eating and talking normally. A boy on the other side of the room was playing on his iPad. No one had noticed her new companion. *Everything seems normal*, Paige thought, *but nothing about this is normal.*

"It's okay," the lady said. "No one can hear or see me but you."

Nothing about this is okay. But maybe now, I'll get some answers. Paige thought. "You were at the beach house with the others, right?" Paige asked with great excitement in her voice. "I have *so* many questions!" Paige went on to say without giving her new table companion a second to reply.

"Yes, I'm sure you do, and I'll answer your questions, but right now, we need to go to the old church cemetery."

This was not the reply Paige had hoped for. "What?" Paige asked a little louder than she realized; she looked around to see if anyone had heard her. Of course, they had. Every eye in the place was staring at her. She swiftly picked up her book and pretended she was reading out loud. *No one's buying this*, she thought.

"Are you Amethyst?" Paige asked.

"That is correct, you must have found your letter. Are you ready? It will be dark soon."

Paige paid Mrs. Star and walked out of the café. She

and Amethyst walked into the old cemetery just as it was getting dusk. The trees appeared to be getting ready for the night; their branches all covered in moss, waved slowly in the breeze. The graves were all neatly arranged with beautiful old headstones telling the stories of the inhabitants of this little piece of Starfish Island.

"Each headstone tells a story," Amethyst said as she led Paige through the old, ornate gates. The creaking of the gates seemed like something from an old horror movie. Paige thought, *should I be scared or excited?* She laughed quietly to herself.

"There's nothing to be scared of," Amethyst said as if reading her thoughts. "Paige, read each and every headstone. Please don't be in a hurry. The information you will need will be revealed from stone to stone. What you learn here may, when the time comes, save your life and the lives of your friends."

How can reading old headstones save anyone? And what does she mean by saving my friends? Paige's thoughts were interrupted by a sound she'd never heard before. This was not a pleasant sound. The hair on her arms were now standing up with the goose bumps that appeared when she first heard the sound.

"Amethyst, what was that?" Paige asked as softly as she could with a little quiver in her voice.

"We are not the only ones here you cannot see."

"What are you talking about?" Paige asked in a louder voice this time.

"There are others on Starfish Island who are hidden from all of you, Paige. They are demons, and they have plans for everyone living here. But their plans are all evil." Amethyst continued with a new sound of urgency in her voice. "Do not worry, Paige. I am here, and they would not dare to try to harm you. Please, Paige, start reading the headstones. It will take you some time to understand what they mean. But know this—you have been given the ability to accomplish this task."

Paige knew from the letter that there were demons as well as angels on the island. She was very excited about the angels. However, fear would rise up in her when she thought about demons being here as well.

Paige began to read the first headstone; certain words began to glow. "Amethyst, why are these words glowing?" Paige asked with so much excitement in her voice, you could feel it. Amethyst didn't respond. Paige turned around to look for her. *Great! She's disappeared again! You'd think she'd hang around especially now. What was she thinking leaving me with the demons here? She said as long as she was here, the demons wouldn't harm me.*

Oddly, though realizing Amethyst had left, Paige felt a sense of strength and power she hadn't experienced before. *Amethyst's leaving won't stop me from reading as many of these headstones as I can. I'll just write down the glowing words from each stone. Maybe that will give me the information I'll need.*

But that was easier said than done. Not every headstone had words that glowed. Paige had time enough to read only three headstones before it was too dark for her to even make out the names of those buried there. *This will have to wait until tomorrow*, she told herself as she quickly left the old cemetery.

Walking home she wondered how the glowing words on the headstones could help anyone with anything, much less save somebody from harm. She also pondered what Amethyst had told her about the demonic presence and what that had to do with a group of kids. "Why would demons even care about what we are doing?" She said out loud. If she said what she was thinking out loud maybe it would all make sense to her, she reasoned within herself. However, this was not the case. Speaking out loud what she was thinking only made her thoughts seem insane. *If the demons are really so bad, why would Amethyst leave me there alone?* With this last thought of the night's events, Paige decided to just enjoy the walk home.

The air was cool and carried the smell of salt and sand. The night sky was illuminated with an orchestra of twinkling stars and a moon so bright it complimented the melody they were playing. The speculations of all the new information Paige had been given was now neatly tucked away for a later time.

Paige didn't see the many hollowed-eyed demons glaring at her. They came out of nowhere and began to gather all around her. She heard their voices, but she mistook them for the wind rattling the leaves in the trees. Amethyst had not disappeared. She was in a battle with the demons to prevent them from attacking Paige. The demons knew that the knowledge she could obtain from the headstones would be part of their undoing.

CHAPTER 11
Back to School

*T*he sun was shining ever so brightly. The temperature would have been unbearable had it not been for the misty breeze coming briskly across the ocean waves.

"Hurry or we'll be late," I said trying to get the gang off the beach and on their way to school. *How could the summer be over so soon?* I thought.

The others reluctantly gathered their backpacks and headed to school. Walking together as we'd done for many years. As we entered the hallway inside the school, we looked at each other, "Later," was all that was said.

School from all appearance was normal, well that is not exactly true. Normal for all the children except the gang. I had a sense of "knowing" that something was different when we entered the building. The rest of the gang felt something as well. We all turned to look at each other again.

That's when for the first time we saw the guardian angels together

somewhere other than the beach house. It was even more exciting because standing by each member of the gang was an angel. Their appearance wasn't as before; there was something majestic about them. We noticed that when we looked at the angels' shadows, they had wings. Not little wings but large, magnificent, feathery wings neatly tucked behind their backs but not noticeable from the front.

Michael wanted to say something to the one standing to his left, but before he could get his thoughts into words, they all disappeared. But this time was different; they did not just vanish as before, they gradually faded into the back ground of the school telling Paige, Michael, Lee, Allen, and me, "We are here should you need us."

The gang was unaware of the demons who were working desperately to give the gang problems any way they could. One demon tried the age-old trick of having the meanest kid on the playground bully Lee during recess. That might have worked in times past, but not that day. Gary, Lee's guardian angel, was right there.

The meanest kid's name was Charlie. Charlie wasn't a bad kid, but he was easily influenced by the little demons that hung around him. They would whisper in his ears ever so softly. Charlie had yet to meet any angels or even any humans who cared enough about him to help him understand good from evil. He thought those soft whispers were coming from friends, and that made Charlie smile.

"Hey Lee," Charlie said in a stern almost angry voice, "that swing you're on is mine. You better be out of it by the time I get there, you hear me?"

Charlie started running full speed in Lees' direction. Lee was making haste to get out of Charlies' path. That's when Gary made himself known to the demon speaking to Charlie. Lee stared in wonderment of the elegant creature appearing right before him. Gary had always appeared as a gentle, older man, but right then, he was the size of the Empire State Building, and his wings seemed to stretch across the whole playground. Gary displayed his true, majestic, spiritual being of great wonder. The demon who was influencing Charlie ran like a scared puppy, and Charlie stopped within inches of Lee.

Lee just sat in the swing waiting for Charlie's next move. Lee thought that Charlie appeared confused and sad. Lee got out of the swing and held it for Charlie. A brief smile of kindness showed on Charlie's face as he said, "Thank you." Gary faded into the background as before but not before he winked at Lee and said, "Good job, Lee. Kindness is what Charlie needs. You have planted a seed in Charlie that someone else will water and make grow."

Charlie was an only child, a "mistake," at least that's what his parents had told him. Charlie's dad drank a lot, and his mom barely had any time for him. Charlie had learned that his parents would notice him only when he got into trouble. To Charlie having his parents take notice of him for any reason made him feel loved. He also had noticed that when he was good, neither of his parents took notice or had any time for him. He felt that negative attention from his parents was better than no attention at all; he felt it was a form of love.

Paige walked into her classroom, she was happy that school had started again. She always enjoyed learning new things, and this was her favorite subject, science. She stopped shortly inside the room; a new girl was sitting in her favorite seat. *What to do?* She immediately thought about going to the girl and setting her straight about whose desk she was at. This thought had barely come into her mind when she noticed Amethyst standing by the new girl with her mighty wings extended to full length. Paige immediately, looked around to see if anyone else had noticed Amethyst. The other students were talking and catching up on each other's summer activities. No one seemed to notice anything except their friends. Paige's initial impulse about the new girl was replaced with a kinder, gentler one. She walked over to the new girl. "Hi. My name is Paige," she said with a friendly smile. "May I sit at this desk beside you?"

"My name is Sally Waters. It would be great if you sat here. At least I would know one of my classmates," she said with a friendly laugh.

Paige was totally unaware of the demonic presence in her classroom. She knew her first thought concerning the new girl had been wrong. She also knew it was not like her to be mean or unfriendly to anyone, especially a new classmate. She soon forgot about the unpleasant thoughts she'd had earlier. Not only was science her favorite subject; her teacher this year was one she truly admired. She was soon lost in the world of science.

The school bell ringing startled Michael, who had been deep in thought about the summer and especially the night he was allowed in the house with the angels. He so wanted to share what he had learned with the gang, but even they might not have believed him, he thought, and he could not, would not chance losing their friendship.

When that first day of school ended, the gang left their classrooms knowing they would meet up on their walk home.

Running as fast as his feet could take him, Allen was trying to catch up with Lee. *Lee always walks fast even when he walks slow*, Allen thought. *Does that even make sense? Ahh, who cares?* "Hey Lee," Allen yelled hoping that would get Lee's attention at least long enough to slow Lees' pace a bit. It worked. Lee turned in Allen's direction and saw Allen closing the gap between them. "Wait up, Lee! What do you think about the new girl in school today?" Allen went on as if they were already having a conversation.

"What new girl?" Lee asked, not really caring about any new girl.

"A new family moved to Starfish Island, and you'll never guess what their names are. I will even give you a hundred tries, because you will never guess." Allen went on and on.

Paige, Michael, and I joined them. "Lee's trying to guess the name of the new family in town," Allen said with a smug look on his face.

"Waters," Paige replied. "Sally Waters is in my class. She's the daughter of the Mr. Waters who was looking at the beach house."

That was not good news for the gang. We all wondered how we would solve the mystery of the beach house if it was sold to Mr. Waters.

We walked in silence for a while. I broke the silence. "We'll all meet at the beach right after supper."

The others agreed and went their separate way home.

Paige's granddad was waiting for her as she came running through the back door. "What's the hurry, Paige?" he asked although he knew the answer before he even asked the question. Things were always the same after school— the gang would do their homework and then their chores, have dinner with their families, and head to the beach until their parents made them come home. Paige's granddad was glad she had such a good group of kids to hang out with, and it was nice, he thought, that all the parents were friends. But today he had a big surprise for Paige, and he couldn't wait to show her.

"Wait just a minute, young lady. Don't you think you could at least give your granddad a hug when you see him?"

Paige's face blushed with joy and love for her granddad. He was so precious to her. She loved her parents very much, but her granddad had always had a very special place in her heart. She threw her arms around his neck as he stooped down to give her a hug.

"Wait until you see what I found!" he said. He took her by the hand and headed to his antique store. He was excited to share his find with his granddaughter; they had always had a special connection. The first time he'd held her in his arms, he knew they would have a special bond, one not seen with human eyes.

"Remember when you were asking me about the furniture shipment I received last month? I finally got a reply from the shipping company. The furniture apparently belonged to an old family that used to live here on Starfish Island, Steve and Judy Heinrich. Well, at one time it belonged to the family, but it was sold at auction when the couple passed away. They said that their company had received a letter and payment in full for all the furniture and that it was to be sent to my store."

He handed Paige a receipt for the furniture. "They didn't have any more information about who had paid for or requested it be shipped here. It's a big mystery. It really doesn't belong to me, so I can't sell it. Strange, eh?"

CHAPTER 12
Andrew's Dreams

I laid in bed thinking about nothing in particular; but for some strange reason, I couldn't fall asleep. Sleep used to be so easy. I'd normally close my eyes, and the next thing I'd hear was Mom telling me breakfast was ready. I could even smell the great aromas that would fill the air each time Mom was preparing the next great feast that was spread so delightfully on our dining room table. Each meal would be a presentation of her love for her family.

I'll miss this when I'm away at college. College? That's so far away from the reality of my life right now. Andrew continued to talk aloud his thoughts, not that he expected someone to answer, he just felt it was better if he said it out loud as opposed to thinking it. *Or is this really a dream? When I wake up, will my life be as it was before we saw the angels? Be that as it may, things had changed! If I just lie here, keep my mind blank, and close my eyes, next thing, it'll be morning. No big deal, right?*

Nothing could have been further from the truth, and I knew that. For the last few nights, every time I closed my eyes expecting a good night's rest, I'd received anything but. As soon as my eyes closed, I was carried away into an unknown world, one full of mystery and surprise. I wasn't afraid of what I saw because it was most enjoyable. It was what I had been told and shown about me and my future that made me quite anxious.

Just as he began to drift off to sleep he spoke quietly to himself, "maybe tonight will be just a normal night of sleep."

"Andrew, Andrew, it's okay. Open your eyes. You are not in any danger." Jewel, one of the angels was speaking, but I didn't want to open my eyes, I just wanted to sleep.

Jewel spoke softly. "Please understand, Andrew, that you are very important to our God. We have no desire to hurt you. We are here only to help you learn and understand what your mission is, that's all. Once you understand, we will be able to just whisper to you when you are awake, and you will hear us.

"Sometimes, God uses dreams to guide you to the truth. He realizes that you have hopes and dreams of your own for your life, and this is all part of God's plan. For you to choose. But sometimes, your plans and His do not agree. That is when He will give you dreams and visions of what could be if you followed the path He chose for you.

"It's not that your dreams are wrong or bad. He sees your life from beginning to end. He knows what is best for you and those you will meet along the way. You see, Andrew, He intertwines your life with the lives of others and will make you interact when the time is right. Like trains leaving a station and coming back to the station. Do you understand what I am saying?"

"Yes," I replied. "Why didn't you just say that the first time you were here?"

I thought of the first time I had seen Jewel; she was in a large crowd of people. At least I thought they were people then, but I'd learned they were angels. They were all singing in an unfamiliar language, but even without understanding the words, I felt a great peace.

Lights were emanating from the angels in the crowd—beautiful, bright, celestial colors that engaged each other in a magical dance that would fill the air with excitement and wonder. There were colors I had never seen before. I remembered thinking how guys weren't really into colors unless they were the colors of their favorite teams. That thought again made me chuckle.

I had listened and watched the angels moving ever so gracefully in a spiritual way. A large stage at the front of the room got my attention. I moved slowly though the crowd; I wanted to take in all the wonders that were being unveiled right before my eyes. I moved closer to the stage and saw the person leading the heavenly praise and worship. To my great surprise, that person was me!

CHAPTER 13
The Oak Tree

*L*ee stood just beneath the big oak tree he had climbed earlier that year. The tree was even larger than he remembered. This was the tree that allowed him to see the harbor and all the ships resting in the docks at the pier. But the harbor and ships were not on his mind as he glanced up trying to see the top of the tree or at least the branch he had perched on that day.

The branches appeared to be stretching toward the sky and swaying ever so slightly in the cool breeze coming across the ocean. The waving branches reminded him of the congregation at church on Sundays when the people would praise and worship God. Lee wondered if trees worshipped anything, and then he thought how crazy that idea was. He just smiled at the thought of trees, birds, and the rest of nature worshipping God.

If I stay here long enough, will he come back? Was all Lee could think about.

He so wanted to tell the others how he had gotten down the tree so fast and without harm. "When I think of how I just floated down from that big limb I was sitting on," Lee said out loud. "Just like a leaf leaving a tree when the wind blows too hard. Who'd believe me?" Lee continued talking out loud as if he was talking to someone else as opposed to what he really was doing, talking out loud to himself. "Sometimes, I don't even believe what happened myself, and I was there!" A smile came across his face as he thought about that moment and how it felt so natural just floating in the air.

He relaxed on the cool green grass that grew all around the tree. He laid on his back with his arms under his head and his legs crossed, not a care in the world. Looking up through the branches he got a glimpse of the blue sky and the birds soaring through the air. *One day, I'll soar across the sky, darting to and fro between the clouds. Or maybe I'll land on one of the larger clouds and just watch the world below.* He watched seagulls soaring ever so eloquently across the backdrop of the sky. His continued to think of how cool it would be to soar high above everyone and everything. *What a view they must have of the whole world, not just this little harbor and the ships!* He closed his eyes as he smiled at the thought of soaring like an eagle. He was soon fast asleep.

He was awakened suddenly by the sound of the foghorn, but that was not all that had drawn him from his peaceful sleep. Lee stood up as if he had been pushed up by something beneath him propelling him upward and landing him on his feet.

"Please do not be afraid, Lee. I am not here to hurt you," a voice said.

"How do you know my name? Who are you? One of the angels? How did you fly me down from the tree when I was stuck up there, I mean, before I started down on my own and—"

"Lee, take a deep breath. Relax. I will answer all your questions, one by one. First of all, let me introduce myself. In your world, I'm called Gary. It's so nice to finally be able to meet you face to face."

"What are you?"

"That's a very good question. I am a heavenly spiritual being. Your world sometimes calls us guardian angels. All of us you saw at the beach house, as you call it, are guardian angels."

"Why are you here?" Lee said with a little apprehension in his voice.

"Do not be afraid." Gary said, feeling the heighten anxiety that Lee was now experiencing. "We are all here to help."

"Help, what do you mean help, like with my homework and chores?" The apprehension that was heard in his voice just moments ago was now replaced with excitement. This was a welcoming thought, *someone to help me with my chores, cool!*

Gary broke into laughter that was so jolly that Lee could not help but to laugh out loud with him.

"No, not with your homework or chores," Gary said, with a very serious look of concern on his face. "We are here to protect all of you until you learn how to protect yourselves."

That wasn't the answer Lee had been hoping for. In fact, that thought had never crossed his mind.

"What are you talking about, Gary?" Lee said a little more boisterous then he meant too. This is the safest place on planet earth." He continued as if he needed to remind Gary of his current location.

"Yes, you are right, Lee, if we are talking about humans and this nice place you call home. I am not talking about protecting you from humans. Gary went on to say in a calm manner trying not to frighten Lee. Other spiritual beings are here besides us, but they are not your friends. They are demonic beings whose job is to keep you from completing your mission. At school the other day, did you see that each member of your gang had an angel beside him or her?"

"Yes. I saw you standing next to me. And on the playground when Charlie wanted to take the swing from me, you changed into this enormous creature."

"Lee, as you see me now is how we appear to you, so you will not be frightened. How you saw me on the playground is how angels really look. God made each one of us for a special task. However, all angels are powerful heavenly spiritual beings. Charlie is not a bad kid. He was being influenced by a demon you could not see or hear. That demon needed to know whom he was dealing with, and I am afraid this; Gary pointed to himself, will not scare anyone."

Gary and Lee broke into such joyful laughter that even the birds stopped singing to listen to the joyous sound.

Gary continued to explain to Lee why the angels where there. He told Lee that all the members of the gang had angels assigned to look after them and assist them when asked.

"We are here to protect each one of you! Just know Lee, you are never alone, and you will learn how to defeat the demons before the real battle begins."

Just like that, Gary was gone.

CHAPTER 14
The New Girl

*A*s the water crashed against the shore, the gang made their way along the rocky edge of the inlet water pool. It was a path they had taken many times before; it was their private meeting place. Once they were around the curve ahead, they could no longer be seen by anyone on the beach or in the ocean.

This secret place they would later learn is where they would understand the reason they and only a select few of the town folks could see the people that first appeared to them at the beach house.

"No, I don't like what you're suggesting at all," Michael said to Paige as they all got to the shore around the pool of the clearest blue water you will ever see.

"What's going on between you two?" I asked.

Paige began to tell me of her wonderful idea. Michael walked right up between us looking directly at Paige.

He began to share all the reasons he believed Paige's idea was insane. "Paige thinks we should invite Sally Waters into our gang, and I say absolutely not! That's the craziest idea I've ever heard!" Michael went on and on.

I walked slowly past Michael to Paige, who was now sitting on a rock by the water.

"I just thought," Paige began slowly as if she had just been scolded by her parents, "that if we let her in just enough to find out what she knows about the old beach house, maybe she would tell us why her dad wants to buy it, that's all."

"That's brilliant!" I said. "We won't bring her here or any other place that's special to us. We befriend her just long enough to get the information we need."

Lee and Allen had been skipping pebbles across the pool, waiting for our debate to be over. "Well, if she seems real cool, we could let her into the gang," Allen said. "She *is* very pretty." Allen looked as if he were in a trance when he spoke about Sally. The trance was broken by the loud laughter from the rest of the gang. This made his face turn red as a ripe tomato.

"I was planning to go over to her house later today. My mom baked them a pie to say, 'Welcome to Shell Cove,' as she put it. That'll open the door for me to ask questions and not appear as if I really care about her answers," Paige told the gang.

"That's most excellent!" Michael said.

The gang turned to Michael, who had been all against the plan just seconds earlier.

"What? A fellow can't change his mind?" Michael asked as he shrugged his shoulders.

Paige turned to leave and told the gang she'd give them an update tomorrow.

Walking down the sidewalk that would lead her to Sally's house, she enjoyed the smell of the flowers, the birds singing, and the cool breeze of course coming in from the ocean. She entered the yard though an ornate gate that reminded her of the one at the old cemetery. As she got closer to Sally's house, she had a revelation. *How could I have lived here my whole life and never noticed this before? Sally's house is exactly like the old beach house!*

Well, not exactly like it. Sally's house still has paint on it, and the shutters were all in place. In fact, the house had been so well maintained that it looked almost new. But it too did not look as if it belonged on an island. It had seven gables and wide steps that led to a porch that wrapped around the entire house. Of course, it also had a beautiful porch swing and an enormous front door. Paige wondered why Mr. Waters wanted to buy another house just like the one he was living in.

She walked up the wide steps and was immediately greeted by Sally, who was on the porch swing reading.

"Hi, Paige. It's so nice of you to stop by," Sally said.

She was more than overjoyed to see Paige. Since their first meeting at school, Sally felt that Paige and she would become friends, maybe even best friends.

Paige extended her mother's pie she was holding to Sally. "My mom baked this to say, 'Welcome to Shell Cove.'"

"That's very thoughtful of your mom. Please tell her we'll enjoy every bite. Since my mom passed away, my dad does most of the cooking. He's not a bad cook, but he never makes desserts. This pie will be a real treat for us. Would you like to come in and have some pie with us now?"

That was exactly what Paige had hoped for; not only would she get to talk with Sally, but she'd get to talk to Sally's dad as well.

Sally opened the door and invited Paige in. "My dad's in his library," Sally said as the girls made their way down the large hall. Paige was taking in all the lovely décor room after room—overstuffed chairs, crystal chandeliers, paintings, and other items that told a story of their homeland, England. Paige had a strange feeling that she had seen all this before or at least some of it, but she couldn't remember where. She wanted to clear her mind of everything except finding out what Mr. Waters knew about the old beach house and why he wanted to buy it.

Sally stopped outside her dad's library to inform him of their guest and let him know she'd be serving the pie in a few minutes. Her dad's lovely old library was full of books new and extremely old and rare. The bookcase was cherry-red mahogany that hugged the wall and extended to the twelve-foot ceiling. A ladder attached to a brass rail allowed him to reach any book on any shelf regardless how high the shelf was. "There's nothing like holding the words of the writer in your hand and the smell of the paper and ink infusing every breath you take as you wait for the story to unfold," Sally's dad would tell visitors to his library.

Paige wanted to go into the library but didn't want to be too pushy on her first visit. She thought it would be best if she followed Sally as opposed to touring the magnificent home on her own.

Paige was amazed at all the antique furnishings in the kitchen. Sally had noticed Paige's admiring looks at her home the minute she had invited her in. She waited for Paige to say something, but Paige was silent, at least for now. Sally served the pie with vanilla ice cream, and Mr. Waters joined the girls in the breakfast nook.

Paige had nothing but questions. And Mr. Waters was more than happy to answer them. However, Paige lost focus of her mission; she asked about the house and its furnishings rather than about Mr. Waters's interest in the old beach house.

He had fallen in love with the house when he had seen it during his first visit to Starfish Island and had purchased it. The house reminded him of some old houses in England. Most of furniture had been handed down through the generations. He had bought a few pieces at estate sales, but his library was his pride and joy. He had collected books since he was a small child. "Books keep us alive," he said. "They take us to places we'll never travel to and give us adventures we wouldn't have without them."

Once the dessert was finished, Paige and Sally did

the dishes and Mr. Waters retreated to his library and the adventure awaiting him.

Paige said, "I didn't realize how long I've been here. I hope I haven't overstayed my welcome."

"Don't be silly, Paige. It was great that you came by. And please tell your mom we loved the pie. Please thank her for us."

"Of course. I must be heading home now. Thanks for the great company. Your dad is an excellent host, and so are you. Before I forget, I want to invite you to go to the beach with my friends and me this Saturday if you're not busy."

"Really?" Sally said enthusiastically. "I'd love to, Paige!"

"Great. It's settled. I'll come by for you around nine on Saturday morning. All you'll need is a bathing suit, a beach towel, and maybe some suntan lotion."

The girls walked together until they reached the gate. Paige said, "Goodbye! See you tomorrow at school."

Sally agreed and the girls parted ways. She found herself skipping like a little schoolgirl all the way back to the porch. She was joyfully singing as she entered through the front door. Her dad smiled as he listened to his daughter singing all the way passed his library and up the stairs to her room. Just a few moments later, Sally came down and entered the library. She gave her dad a big hug and a kiss on his cheek. She told him goodnight and headed back upstairs to her room.

Sleep for Sally was sweet that night. She no longer felt alone.

CHAPTER 15
The Meeting

$\mathcal{A}$ll the gang were talking cheerfully about nothing in particular as they entered the opening to their secret place. It had always been a special place for them hidden from the rest of the island.

"The air in here always smells so fresh and salty," Paige said looking around at the beautiful waterfall that fell softly into the crystal-blue water below.

No one said a word; the angels were there in their secret place. It seemed at first as if they didn't expect to see them there. But when the older man approached Andrew, it was very clear that they had been waiting on the gang.

If Andrew was afraid, he showed no outward signs. It was apparent he had seen them all before and maybe knew them.

"Good to see you again, Andrew. Have you thought much about our last meeting?"

With this exchange of words, the rest of the gang looked at each other in complete surprise; they couldn't believe

what they were hearing. They realized I had a meeting with the angels but hadn't shared that with the them.

"Wait just a minute!" Michael said with all the authority he could rally.

The man turned to Michael and grinned. His eyes were sparkling. He said, "Michael, you and I will finish our conversation later. Right now, we must talk with Andrew."

He and I walked toward the other angels as Paige, Michael, Lee, and Allen stood there in disbelief. It was clear by the way I was at ease with the angels that it wasn't our first meeting. *But when had Andrew gone to the old beach house without the rest of them?* they wondered.

"Guys, there's something I've been wanting to tell you," Paige said, "and now seems to be the right time." She turned to the angels who were standing near Brian and me. "See the young lady to the left of the adults?"

"Yes!" Allen, Michael, and Lee said in harmony.

"Tell us," Michael said with his hands on his hips and a stern look, "have you too been meeting at the old beach house with the angels and Andrew?"

"No!" Paige said, emphatically. "You guys know I'd never do that. We're all in this together! Paige continued on with the information she had so wanted to share with the gang, but somehow it had never been the right time. "Remember the day I went to the library after church while the rest of you went to the beach?" The boys shook their heads in agreement. "When I got to the library, I remembered it was closed on Sundays. So, I decided to go to Star café to have a soda. When I walked into the café I sensed the angels were there. I didn't see them at first, just felt their presence, I can't really explain it; I just knew.

"While I was waiting on Mrs. Star to bring me my order, Amethyst appeared at my table. That's right—just appeared out of thin air. She said that she'd been there all along but that I hadn't listened to her or looked for her. At first, I didn't understand what she was trying to tell me."

Paige saw that the boys were hanging on to her every word, and anxiously awaiting her next sentence. For a split second, she wanted to find out how long they'd keep looking at her in silence. Their eyes were wide open, pupils dilated trying to take in everything she was saying.

When Paige had finished her confession, the boys just stared at each other wondering what else had happen between the angels and their gang that hadn't been shared. They have always shared everything with each other. Until the beach house. They stood there in total silence, starring at one another.

Lee broke the silence and got the gangs attention. "The guy beside Amethyst is Gary. He's the reason I was able to get down that big old oak tree last year."

"What?" Michael asked in disbelief.

"Wait," Lee said. "Let me tell you what happened. I was lying under that big tree and fell asleep. I was awakened by Gary. At first, I was scared. I didn't know what to say or do. But he was so cool! He told me he was always available for me and that he watched over me. He said that I could talk to him any time and that he would hear me. He's the best!"

Allen was silent. These last few minutes made him painfully aware he was the only one who had not met with an angel by himself. He desperately wanted to be a part of this new and exciting adventure. Just as he began to feel sorry for himself with his eyes tearing up and his face turning red; a feeling of someone or something touched his arm lightly, as with a feather. He turned expecting to see someone next to him, but no one was there. The others were deep in conversation about their meetings with the angels. *Oh well, it must have been the wind*, Allen thought. At that very moment he felt it again, and that time, he saw him.

"Allen, I've been here all along, but you have been so busy and interested in what the others had seen and done that you just could not open your eyes to see me or your ears to hear me," he said.

Allen's face was no longer the color of a tomato, it had transformed into a bright, almost glowing appearance. He had a new sense of awareness that even the sky seemed bluer. The air had a new fragrance and this time it was not of hamburgers and fries, it was more like a still, yet waving smell of life.

"I am Clarence, but you can call me Clifford. All my friends just call me Clifford."

Clifford handed Allen a pouch. Allen took the pouch, opened it to see what was inside. Much to his surprise, it was empty. "What is this, Clifford? By the way, can I just call you Cliff?" Allen asked with a grin.

"Of course, Allen. Cliff will be just fine. The pouch is to hold your most precious seashells."

"What do you mean? All my seashells are great! But I'm not sure I'd call them precious," Allen said as he tried to change his face to fit the expression he was trying to make. Cliff tried to mimic Allen's expression, and that brought forth a great joy of laughter from both of them.

"Allen, when you have collected the right seashells, you will know they belong in this pouch. It will keep them safe until you need them."

The gang, deep in conversation, had forgotten that I was on the other side of the crystal blue pool talking with the angels

Brian wanted to talk with me concerning my dreams—what I saw and how I felt about everything. I was just as excited to talk with Brian; I had so many questions. However, Jewel spoke. "Andrew, you seem to be relaxed but at the same time excited about seeing us here."

I was at first shy about revealing my thoughts about what I had seen and heard over the past few months, but I was excited about telling them I had talked with God personally.

My thoughts turned to my meeting with God.

"Come in, Andrew. Please take the seat right here next to me."

Andrew stood as still as a statue; his mouth was wide open in amazement at the splendor before his eyes. He continued to look around the great room, and took in the magnificent lights, colors, and sounds. The entire room was like nothing he had ever seen before. To Andrew's amazement, animals that were natural enemies in the wild were sitting or walking around the room in perfect peace one with the other. A large lion was lying next to a young lamb that was sleeping peacefully, unaware of the potential danger right next to him. However, in this place the lamb had nothing to fear from the king of the jungle. Andrew looked up expecting to see a ceiling; instead, he saw only sky. It was a velvety purple, and the stars twinkled with brilliant colorful sparks of light that shot back and forth to each other in a heavenly conversation.

He turned to the sound of gently flowing water coming from the most magnificent waterfall he had ever seen. Each drop of water glowed, even glistened as it mingled with the others in a playful dance from the top of the waterfall until it reached the sparkling, aqua-green pool below. The rocks around the pool were making a joyful praise to God, as the plants swayed with their leaves outstretched as they too were praising God to the music of the water. The aromas flooding the room reminded Andrew of a mixture of saltwater, sand and sun on a midafternoon at the beach.

"Andrew!"

Startled by hearing his name, his attention immediately turned toward the person sitting on a throne. "A rainbow that shone like an emerald encircled the throne." Revelation 4:3 The man on the throne had hair so white that it was almost translucent, and moved gently in a soft breeze that was floating through the room. His eyes were crystal-blue with a sparkle that seemed to see right through Andrew, yet a kindness Andrew could feel.

"Yes sir," Andrew said so quietly that his words were barely audible. He moved quickly toward the man with an overwhelming feeling of excitement.

"Please sit right here beside me. The man motioned to the chair that was placed beside the throne. I've waited a long time for this very moment," the man said.

"What do you mean, sir?"

"You see Andrew, I have been around since the beginning of time. He smiled. Actually, I created time. You are here because I ordained this meeting from the beginning, even before you were born."

Andrew's mouth was wide open, but that time, it was in disbelief.

"You seem to be wondering if I'm a crazy ol' man. Some have called me worse," he said with a sad look that made Andrew's heart feel heavy. "You see, Andrew, I created everything."

Thoughts were racing through Andrew's mind. Ever since he could remember, he felt—no, he knew—that there had to be someone or something that had been there from the beginning and had made the world and everything in it. *Could this really be Him?* "Who are you?" Andrew asked.

"I AM that I AM." Exodus 3:14

Andrew knew from his dad that that reply could mean only one thing—the man on the throne was not a man at all, but God.

"I've heard my dad, who's a pastor, talk about You on Sundays. Why am I here? Why would You want to speak to me? I'm nobody, just a teenager living in Shell Cove hoping to one day be a world-champion swimmer. I'm not what people would call religious."

"You can stop now, Andrew. I know all about you. That's right. I created you. I knew you in your mother's womb. I have plans for you, plans to prosper you, good plans, and no plans to harm you. And whatever I plan always comes to pass."

"What shall I call you? My heart feels that what You're saying is true."

The man didn't reply to Andrew's question; instead he had questions of his own.

"Did your pastor tell you about My Son?"

"Yes, he did, Sir. My dad said You sent Your Son here so we could live forever with You and Him."

"What do you think about that?"

"If You are Who You say You are, Sir, You already know what I think about Your Son."

"On July 24, 2005, you, Andrew, told My Son you believed in Him and what He had done. You also told Him you would do whatever He asked."

Andrew could not believe what he was hearing. *Does this man really know my every thought? Does he know what I'm thinking right now?*

The man smiled, and they laughed so loud that the others in the room looked at them in amazement.

"Andrew, you may call me Abba Father."

"Andrew, Andrew!" Brian asked. "You seem lost in thought."

"Sorry. I was thinking about my meeting with God."

"Andrew, do you think you can help prepare the gang, as you like to call yourselves?"

"I'll do my very best, sir," I replied.

"This is an enormous task you will be undertaking, Andrew," Brian said. "However, all of you have been given individual missions that when put together will outmaneuver the enemy. Remember, Andrew—they will look to you for leadership, so please read everything I have given you. Study each chapter as if your life depended on it, because it will."

Brian and I discussed my role in this new adventure. The rest of the gang were engaged in conversations with their new friends—Jewel, Amethyst, Gary, Clifford, and Marti.

CHAPTER 16
The Shopping Trip

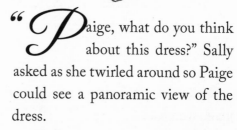

"*P*aige, what do you think about this dress?" Sally asked as she twirled around so Paige could see a panoramic view of the dress.

"Now why are we looking for new dresses? What's wrong with the ones we already have, Sally?"

"There is nothing wrong with our old dresses. But sometimes, don't you feel like dressing up in something new?"

"Yeah, I guess so, but I'd rather be at the beach with the gang than here looking at dresses." Paige said with the expression she made when she was really bored with her current surroundings and longed to be at the special place that always brought her peace and joy no matter what else was going on.

Paige looked at Sally's dress again. Sally didn't say a word, but Paige saw that her remark had hurt Sally. She felt she had some mending of feelings to do especially now that Sally was more than an experiment on gathering information on Sally's dad and his interest in the old beach house. Sally was now her friend and part of the gang.

"Sally, that's a wonderful dress, and it looks even better with you in it." Paige said as she gave her friend a quick hug and said, "I'm sorry."

Sally went to a rack of dresses she had browsed through earlier. "This one will look especially wonderful on you as well."

The dress was a lovely teal green; it had spaghetti straps and was low cut in the back. White ruffles bordered the hem, which had small sea shells that sparkled when she twirled, which made the ruffles appear to be whitecaps on the ocean. They laughed as Sally showed Paige how the dress would be so much fun to wear. She twirled holding the dress close to her as if she were wearing it.

Sally smiled. She knew Paige would look radiant in that color; it would make her eyes sparkle even more, she thought, as she handed Paige the dress to try on. Paige thanked Sally, but her heart wasn't into shopping anymore. Reluctantly she headed to the dressing room.

That was very hateful of your friend to say she would rather be with the gang than you. I thought you were part of the gang! And look at how she's acting about trying on that beautiful dress you took all that time to find just for her. You'd think she'd be more grateful! Sally heard the voice in her head.

Sally never questioned where such thoughts came from; she did feel betrayed by someone she had called a friend. She quickly changed back into her clothes and left the store.

As she hurried home, she didn't notice the beauty of the yellow roses or the different shades of green in the trees; she didn't hear the sweet melody the birds were singing. Her hurt feelings overwhelmed her senses.

Paige came out of the dressing room to show Sally the dress, which was indeed perfect. She did a little twirl and then looked for Sally. "Where are you?" Paige asked.

Ms. Donna, one of the saleswoman said, "Your friend left abruptly. I think that she might have been crying."

Paige quickly changed into her clothes and rushed out to try to find Sally.

"Is there anything I can assist you with?" Ms. Donna asked.

"No thank you." Paige replied as she rushed through the revolving doors.

Once Sally was back home and in her bedroom, the horrible feelings that had consumed her lifted slightly. *Why would I have such horrible thoughts about Paige? She'd never do anything to hurt me, not intentionally anyway. She must think I'm awful for just leaving her there especially since it had been my idea to go shopping.*

Before Sally could call Paige to apologize, the doorbell rang. "I'll get it," Sally yelled at her dad as she ran downstairs and past her dad's library.

Paige waited at Sally's door for what seemed an eternity but was in fact mere seconds. Sally looked out the window and saw Paige, which thrilled her. Sally opened the door, and they started speaking at once.

"Can you ever forgive me, Sally? I can be so selfish at times."

"No, Paige. I was the selfish one leaving you alone in the shop without saying a word. I'm so sorry for that."

Before Paige could translate the remainder of her thoughts into words., Sally wrapped her arms around her so tightly, almost cutting off her air supply.

They hugged and said, "I accept your apology!" Their faces radiated with joy and a great peace embraced them.

"Paige, let's go up to my room," Sally said as she leaned in closer to Paige. "I need to share something with you."

The girls walked slowly past Mr. Waters' library; Paige stopped briefly to say hello. She was much like Mr. Waters when it came to books, especially old ones. Mr. Waters was lost in the adventures of a novel, but he managed a slight wave in acknowledgment of Paige. Paige smiled; she understood how people could get lost for hours in a good book. She wondered if Sally's dad imaged himself as part of the story as opposed to just reading the words. *Does his mind race ahead of the characters trying to unravel the story before it's time, or does he allow the story to unfold as the author intended?*

Sally was halfway up the stairs when she noticed Paige was still looking into the library. "Paige, come on," Sally said loudly enough to get her attention but not enough to disturb her dad.

Paige immediately turned and ran up the stairs to Sally's room. Sally was in her favorite chair, an overstuffed, wingback chair covered in red roses and with large claw feet made of cherry wood. Paige enjoyed the furniture that filled each and every room of the house. Sally and her dad had moved from England last year and Starfish Island was now their new home. They brought a little bit of Ole England with them, it was apparent by the way each and every room told of their English lifestyle.

Paige could tell by Sally's expression that she was frightened by whatever it was she wanted to share. She quickly moved across the hardwood floor to the matching chair Sally was sitting in. She sat down, made herself comfortable, and gave her friend her undivided attention.

"Paige, this may sound very strange to you, but I really hope you believe me."

Sally's body language, and the shear nervous energy emanating from her, told Paige this was serious. "Of course, I'll believe you." She took Sally's hand to reassure her friend that she was there for her.

Sally began to share with Paige the events of the morning. "When I called you this morning about going shopping today, I had a strange sensation that you really didn't want to go with me even though you agreed. As I began to get ready to meet you, thoughts of you really not wanting to go kept creeping into my head. At first, I just laughed it off. I thought, 'If Paige didn't want to go, she'd have told me. She never has any trouble expressing her opinion, right?'

Paige wanted to interrupt her friend at this point, however Sally never gave her the chance.

Sally continued without noticing that Paige wanted to say something. Sally wanted to get her feelings out, in order to find the peace, she so desperately wanted.

"When we met at the café for coffee and pastry, you appeared as excited as I was about shopping. You see, I'd been to the shop yesterday, so I could pick out a dress I knew you'd love. I know you really like cut-offs and tank tops, but I also know that somewhere in there is a young lady screaming to get out."

With that last remark, the girls broke into such joyful laughter that even Sally's dad heard it in the library. A smile of contentment came across his face. He had sincerely wanted Sally to have a close friend here, for she had left her "best friend ever," in England.

Sally shared with Paige the horrible thoughts that seemed to overwhelm her at the shop. She said she'd became so enraged at what Paige had said about the gang, as if she weren't part of it. Paige again tried to interrupt her friend to say she was sorry for causing her this pain and that she was a member of the gang. Sally never paused to allow Paige to speak, not even one word. Sally had to get this all out, that was all she could think about. Once she emptied herself of all the evil thoughts of the morning, Sally relaxed back into her favorite chair; for she had been perched on its edge the entire time.

Paige had wanted to deny what she was being accused of at first, but as Sally shared her thoughts and feelings, Paige began to feel what Sally had felt. She was realizing that what you say, can and does affect people in a positive or negative way. She didn't feel responsible for how her friend was feeling, but she did feel responsible for what she had said out of selfish desire. Paige remembered the words from one of the studies the gang had that year: Galatians 5:22–23: "But the fruit of the Spirit is love, joy, peace, longsuffering, gentleness, goodness, faith, Meekness, temperance." And Galatians 5:26: "Let us not be desirous of vain glory, provoking one another, envying one another."

Several angels had gathered in Sally's room when she had returned from shopping. They didn't make themselves known to the girls, but they had made themselves known to the little demons who had planted evil thoughts in Sally's mind earlier that day. Sally had opened just a little crack by her negative thoughts of Paige earlier that morning, and that was all the invitation the demons needed to plant their evil scheme in her mind. Not that Sally was possessed by the demons; she was just influenced by them.

Paige didn't go on the defensive as she had wanted to earlier because she realized she had to show her friend love and help her through this new experience. As Paige was trying to recall a passage in the Bible that would shed light on Sally's experience, Sally jumped up and walked quickly over to her bookcase. She picked up her study Bible. She turned to 2 Corinthians 10:3–5 and read, "For though we walk in the flesh, we do not war after the flesh: For the weapons of our warfare are not carnal, but mighty through God to the pulling down of strong holds: Casting down imaginations, and every high thing that exalteth itself against the knowledge of God, and bringing into captivity every thought to the obedience of Christ."

Sally gave Paige her thoughts on what the passage meant and how it could have helped her that morning. "When all the negative thoughts I was having today about you and our friendship hit me, I should have told them to leave in the name of Jesus and replace them with the words of Jesus. Being angry is okay, but when I turned that anger into negative thoughts about you, which in my heart I knew could never be true, I gave place to the devil, and he took full advantage of that. As it says right here in Ephesians 4:26–27, Sally pointed to the scripture as she read it, as if reading it was not enough, she wanted Paige to see the words also. 'Be ye angry and sin not: let not the sun go down upon your wrath: Neither give place to the devil.'"

Paige and Sally radiated with this newfound way of defeating the demons who wanted to take them down bunny trails that would lead them from what God had planned for them.

Together, they read Ephesians 4:32: "And be ye kind one to another, tenderhearted, forgiving one another, even as God for Christ's sake hath forgiven you."

They hugged again. "Let's go to the beach and enjoy the remainder of this day in the sunshine," Sally said.

With a big smile, Paige agreed.

Sally changed into her swimsuit and grabbed her beach bag. Together they went into the library to tell her dad bye and to let him know they were headed to the beach for the remainder of the day. Of course, they would need to make a quick stop at Paige's house, so she too could change for the beach.

The girls arrived at the beach just in time to see the completion of another great sandcastle. Allen and Lee were beaming with pride as they admired their accomplishment. I was riding the waves, and to their surprise, so was Michael. We motioned for Paige and Sally to join us. The girls flipped out their beach towels side by side on the sparkling white, soft sand. They dropped their beach bags on the towels and ran hand in hand to join us in the beautiful, crystal-blue ocean.

CHAPTER 17
The Unsupervised Beach Outing

*A*llen and Lee had made plans the night before to get an early start to their day at the beach. They were going to the beach by themselves.

"As your parents, we feel it's time you two boys have the responsibility of going to the beach without your brothers or sister hanging around." Lee's and Allen's moms had addressed the issue of going to the beach unsupervised for several years. The answer had always been the same: "You're too young to go by yourself."

But not that day. Allen and Lee felt they were going through a rite of passage; they had reached the age of unsupervised fun, and what fun they were going to have! They had spent most of the night texting each other about the day's activities—what toys they wanted to bring, what they would put in their lunch bags, and

what drinks they would pack in their small ice chest. The day would be perfect.

The sky was a gorgeous shade of blue with not a cloud in sight. Birds were singing cheerfully as if they were cheering for the boy's newfound freedom.

Allen and Lee packed all their gear into their beach wagon, and off they went. Nothing and no one would spoil the day for them. They got to their favorite spot on the beach. Unpacked their gear, placed each item in its designated place on the large blanket and raced to the water.

"Yahoo!" screamed Allen as the cold, clear waves lapped against him. Lee dove past him into an oncoming wave. They were soon splashing one another and challenging each other to see who could hold his breath underwater the longest.

When they'd had their fill of the water for a while, they raced each other back to the blanket. Grabbed their beach towels to dry off just enough to sit on the blanket without making it soaking wet. They lay on their backs with legs crossed and looked up at the sky; the sight was fit for a Norman Rockwell painting.

"Allen, do you ever wonder what it would be like to soar through the sky?"

"You mean like in an airplane?"

"No, I mean like a bird. Wouldn't that be great? You could look down on the world below and see things you'd never see out of an airplane window. You could fly close to whatever you wanted to look at and then soar off to your next destination," Lee said. He watched seagulls as they soared gracefully through the air. The look on his face as he watched the birds was one of wonderment at the thought of being able to soar like the birds he was watching so intently.

"That would be cool! Do you think we can fly like that in heaven?" Allen looked at Lee as if Lee would have the answer to such a profound question.

"Don't know for sure, but I'm going to try." A wide grin appeared across Lee's face just thinking about the possibility of flying.

"Lee, do you think Jesus and God can fly?"

"Sure, they can. God made everything, right? So of course, He made it so He and Jesus could fly. If you made everything, wouldn't you be sure to make it so you could fly?"

"I can just see Jesus now soaring way up in the clouds, all around heaven, then all around the world and then back to heaven." Lee had his arms outstretched as he ran all around the blanket as if he was looking down from above. He dropped to his knees as if landing on earth. The boys rolled in the sand laughing so hard that their sides hurt.

Allen stopped laughing when he saw a sparkle in the sand. He immediately ran to check it out. *It might be a special shell!* he thought.

Lee was right behind Allen; he didn't know why they were running. All he knew was that he was having fun.

Allen reached the sparkle that caught his eye and was disappointed. It wasn't even a sea shell, instead it was just a soda can some litterbug had left behind. That made them angry; they cherished their beach and couldn't image why anyone would want to leave trash on the beautiful white sand. Allen picked it up and threw it into a beach garbage can.

The boys raced back to their blanket and sat down for a nice lunch of peanut butter and strawberry jam sandwiches, grape Kool-Aid, potato chips, and cookies of course. But before the boys took even one bite of their lunch, they held hands, bowed their heads, and thanked God for their food and the great island they called home. They said a hearty "Amen!"

"Lee, this is the best lunch ever!"

Lee grinned and shook his head in agreement. He couldn't quite say anything because he'd just taken a big bite of his sandwich.

With full bellies, the boys again lay on their blanket with hands behind their heads, their legs crossed, and looking up at the sky. Within minutes, they were fast asleep. But their peaceful bliss didn't last long. They were rudely awakened by a splash of cold water. When the cold water hit Allen's face, he felt as if he were drowning and screamed for help.

His reaction made the culprit who had thrown the water beam with accomplishment; he'd received the response he had hoped for. At least from Allen.

Lee's response was not at all what the culprit had hoped for. Lee came up swinging and hit Charlie right between the eyes. Charlie fell backward and landed on the remainder of Allen's and Lee's lunches. When Lee realized what had actually happened, he went to help Charlie up.

"Can't you take a joke?" exclaimed Charlie while holding his nose that had received the brunt of Lee's punch.

Lee wrapped some ice from the ice chest in a napkin and handed it to Charlie. "I'm very sorry, Charlie. I really didn't mean to hurt you, but you took me totally by surprise. Here put that on your nose."

Charlie took the ice and placed it against his nose, very gently; the punch had hurt.

"I've been watching you guys all morning. I just wanted to join in on the fun, that's all," Charlie said. Charlie stood swaying side to side, one hand holding the ice to his nose and the other hand in the pocket of his shorts.

"So why didn't you come over and ask us instead of throwing water on us? That's not how you make friends Charlie, that's how you make enemies," Allen said.

"I'm not really good at making friends," replied Charlie. A very sad look of disappointment in his recent actions came across Charlie's face as he shrugged his shoulders, and with a soft voice, almost too low for the boys to hear, he told Allen and Lee he was sorry. He turned to leave.

"You want him to join us?" Lee asked Allen in a low voice in case Allen said no.

"Not if he's going to act like the old Charlie. That guy was mean."

"Hey Charlie! Hold on," Lee shouted.

Charlie turned around slowly; he was trying to hide the

tears that had formed in his eyes. He had realized that his actions might have lost him a friend. Not just any friend, but a brand-new friend that he thought really cared about him. Someone who had been nice to him on the playground even after Charlie had been so mean to him.

Charlie turned to face Lee. "I said I was sorry, and I meant it," Charlie said. "What more do you want me to say?" He slowly turned back in the direction to head home.

"Charlie, Allen and I want you to join us," Lee said. "All you have to say is yes."

"Lee, please don't joke about this. I'm really sorry. I just wasn't thinking about how you two would feel being woken up by cold water. It just seemed like a fun thing to do when I went and got the water."

"If we hadn't been asleep, it would have been fun. Well, maybe not on the blanket where all our gear was," Lee said with a chuckle.

"Come on and join us," Allen said. "We're going back into the water!"

The three boys raced each other to the water. Together they would continue this day of unsupervised fun, which would consist of swimming, building sandcastles, and collecting seashells of course.

In the unseen world of the demons, much activity was stirring. One of the lesser demons, Tpmetnoc, was standing in front of Raef and reporting the latest developments in the assignment Raef had given him. Tpmetnoc was to spy on the gang, one member in particular—Allen. Allen was very important to Raef because Allen was the keeper of the pouch.

Allen hadn't fully realized what his task entailed, however, it had become more apparent when he found the first special seashell Cliff had told him about. When Allen picked up the shell, he knew instantly that it belonged in the pouch. Once Allen opened the pouch, the shell seemed to float into the pouch resting carefully in the pocket that looked as if it had been designed especially for it. Tpmetnoc knew this was what his boss had sent him to observe. He couldn't wait to share this news with Raef.

"What do you mean you left immediately after that kid put the shell into the pouch?" Raef yelled. Thick, dark, foul-smelling smoke was coming out of Raef's mouth with each word he blasted at Tpmetnoc. Tpmetnoc was shaking as Raef paced around him. The longer he paced, the larger he became. Tpmetnoc was sure that at any moment he would be sent straight to hell. However, Raef had other plans.

"Was this the first shell that went into that pouch?" Raef asked glaring down at Tpmetnoc with a slight smile on his demonic face.

"Yes, boss," replied Tpmetnoc, who was trembling and hoping that Raef had not noticed the state of fright he was in.

"Are you sure?" Raef walked closer to Tpmetnoc, so close that Tpmetnoc felt Raef's hot breath with each word.

"Yes, boss. I haven't left that kid's side since you assigned me this task. I take my assignments very seriously, sir."

"Yes, yes yes Stop sucking up! You're already a very poor example of a demon. Don't make it any worse by groveling."

Slowly Raef appeared to be calming down, if that was even possible for a demon. Being calm just didn't fit into their mannerism. But right before Tpmetnoc's fiery-red eyes, Raef's demeanor changed. Raef slowly turned to Tpmetnoc.

Raef's actually smiling! Tpmetnoc thought.

"Have you seen that kid Charlie lately?" Raef asked.

"What do you care about him? He's not part of that gang."

Before Tpmetnoc could release another question, he realized he had said the wrong thing. *If the boss wants information, you dummy, you don't ask why! You just give him the information!* he thought.

In a split second, Raef had his claws into Tpmetnoc. "I feel like tossing you into the lake! You know, the one that burns!" roared Raef.

Tpmetnoc began to plead with Raef, who was so amused by how quickly the little demon he held tightly in his claws had turned from a demon who thought it was a good notion to question his boss into a sniffling little crybaby. *No wonder we're losing the battle between good and evil. With soldiers like this on our side?* thought Raef.

"You get one more chance, Tpmetnoc," Raef said as he

tossed him aside. "Your new assignment is to find Charlie and get him into that gang. Got it?"

"Yes, boss, I got it!"

In a split second Tpmetnoc was gone. He didn't wait around in case Raef changed his mind.

"Etah, front and center," yelled Raef.

"Yes boss!" Etah said wishing he were somewhere else. He'd just witnessed the boss's interaction with Tpmetnoc. Etah thought it would be better for him if he were causing problems for one of the humans instead of standing in front of an angry demon three times his size.

"You know the kids in that so-called gang. Go and keep a watch on the one they call Allen. Don't let him out of your sight, but don't taunt him. Just watch and report back to me the moment he finds another shell, got it?" Raef bellowed out his orders as he laughed to himself about the fear he could instill in his little band of demons. *It makes me all hot inside to see Etah squirm.*

Having received his orders, Etah left immediately. No reason to make the boss angry with him. Etah liked it when he was allowed to just watch the humans. He found them interesting. He was amused by how they would get all upset when they hurt another human's feelings. *What's that all about anyway? It's fun to hurt other people's feelings,* he thought. *Humans are so strange the way they care about each other. Well, at least the way most of them do.* For he knew there were humans who could be as mean as any demon.

The boys raced each other back to the blankets, but that time, there were three of them—Charlie was enjoying the beach outing as well. They were starving, or so they thought. It had been only a few hours since they had enjoyed their lunch. At least Allen and Lee had. That hadn't been the case with Charlie. What Allen and Lee called a normal meal with their families was foreign to Charlie. His family never had meals together; in fact, sometimes, Charlie would go for days without a true meal. That wasn't common knowledge, nor did Charlie want that to be known. He felt that he had found true friends for the first time in his life, and he didn't want them to know certain things about his life for fear they would not want to be his friends anymore.

Allen noticed how Charlie looked at the remainder of their lunch, and wondered if Charlie was hungry. "Hey Charlie, you hungry? We packed plenty," Allen said with a smile.

"No thanks," replied Charlie, though he really wanted a PBJ sandwich.

"Ah come on, Charlie! We can't take this back home or our moms will tell us we weren't responsible because we made too much to eat. This is our first day out without supervision. You have to eat one to help us out, okay?" Allen asked with a wide grin of love and caring. How could Charlie resist such an offer as this?

"Well, all right. I wouldn't want you guys to get into trouble or anything. I mean, if it'll really help you out and all," replied Charlie.

Charlie was standing by the blanket, hands behind his back, twisting slightly from side to side. He couldn't wait to taste the PBJ. Charlie dove for a sandwich, but before he could take his first bite, he was interrupted by Lee.

"Charlie, we always thank God for our food before we eat."

Before Charlie knew it, Allen and Lee were holding his hands with their heads bowed. Charlie bowed his head too just like his new friends. "God, thank You for this beautiful day, the food You have supplied, and especially for our new friend, Charlie," said Lee. Lee and Allen said, a big "Amen!"

Charlie was overwhelmed by a feeling he hadn't had for a very long time. He couldn't explain it; he just knew he enjoyed the way it made him feel inside.

The boys finished off most of the food Lee and Allen had packed, and they were full. Now the three lay on their backs, arms behind their heads, legs crossed—not a care in the world. They talked about how they would soar through the sky if they could fly. They laughed and joked as if they had all been friends for years.

I interrupted them briefly when I came and joined them.

"How's your first day on the beach unsupervised going?" I asked as I plopped down on the edge of their blanket.

"Did Mom send you to spy on us?" Lee asked.

"No way. I've been trying out my new surfboard all morning," I said.

"Sweet!" Charlie said.

"You got that right," I said. "My new board is the sweetest. I never thought I'd enjoy anything as much as I do swimming, however surfing comes in real close, you know what I mean?"

Allen, Lee, and Charlie stared at me with looks that told me they had no idea what I meant. That gave me a new appreciation of the age difference between the younger boys and me.

Lee and Allen continued to enjoy the fun and sun with a new friend while I went back to practicing my newfound sport of surfing.

The demonic realm was busy as well, but not with fun. Etah was nearby observing Allen as ordered by his boss. *I really don't get the boss sending me here to spy on that little kid, Allen,* Etah thought. He had been waiting many years to be used by the boss, and hoping to impress the master. *And this is my assignment? Watching a little boy? I wonder what the master would say if he knew the boss was spending so much negative energy on these kids.* That thought made Etah chuckle demonically. *What other kind of energy would a demon have except for negative?* he thought.

"Etah! What are you doing here?" demanded Tpmetnoc with a look of hatred on his already disgusting face.

"Just following the boss's orders," replied Etah smugly with attitude in his voice.

"That Allen kid is my assignment!" shouted Tpmetnoc as he got up close and personal to Etah.

"You don't frighten me. You know as well as I do that I wouldn't be here unless I'd gotten my orders to be here, so back off," replied Etah as he looked Tpmetnoc right in his fiery-red eyes.

Tpmetnoc backed down. He knew what Etah was saying was true. He had lost the Allen assignment and had been ordered to get that pesky kid Charlie into the gang. Tpmetnoc had on many occasions used little Charlie as a pawn in his games with the humans because Charlie was so easily manipulated. Charlie had never been to church. His dad was an alcoholic, and his mother—well, let's just say she saw only the bad things Charlie did. Charlie had decided that if his mom can only see him or have anything to do with him is when he is bad, then bad he would be. Because his heart longed to have his mother care about him.

Just when Tpmetnoc had decided he'd had enough of Etah, he spotted Charlie playing in the ocean with Allen and Lee. *Well this assignment is good as completed*, thought Tpmetnoc. His thought had just reached his little demonic brain when it was spoiled by Etah.

"Didn't the boss send you to get Charlie into that gang of kids?" asked Etah.

"You know he did," Tpmetnoc said with a smirk.

"Wasn't the boss's plan to have Charlie spy for you and tell you what that bunch of kids were up to?" Continued Etah.

"You act as if you know something. Spill it, you little twerp, or I'll beat it out of you, you got it?" Tpmetnoc yelled.

"Why should I help you?"

That last remark threw Tpmetnoc into a full-blown rage. He went at Etah with every fiber of his demonic being. The two of them battled until they were bruised and bleeding. Foul-smelling smoke and flames were coming out of them.

Etah thought it was the perfect time to rub a little salt into Tpmetnoc's fresh wounds. "Did you see how little Charlie is fitting into that gang?" Etah asked. "Is that what the boss meant when he told you to get little Charlie into the gang?" He smirked. "I don't think so."

Tpmetnoc turned to again attack Etah; his claw-like fingers stretched out to tear into Etah's flesh. Etah had known what he had said would enrage his follow demon and had taken flight before Tpmetnoc could respond. "You think you can escape me, you inferior little demon? You forget I know where you hide!" Laughed Tpmetnoc, with his little evil smile.

If the humans had seen what was happening on their beautiful beach, they would have run away screaming. Fortunately for Allen, Lee, and Charlie, that was not the case. They were still having a great time enjoying their first day at the beach without supervision.

Right now, they were being entertained by watching

dolphins that had made their way very near the shore. The larger dolphins appeared to be showing off the new additions to their families. The larger dolphins would jump high above the baby dolphins and dive into the water right in front of them. The baby dolphins would try doing what they had observed. The show of affection that the larger dolphins had for their offspring made Allen and Lee smile with joy in their hearts. Charlie, however, felt a tinge of sadness. His thoughts turned to his parents, who hadn't shown him even an ounce of what the adult dolphins were showing their little ones. *And they're just dolphins*, Charlie thought.

The dolphins headed out into the ocean. The entertainment they had provided formed more great memories for the three boys. To Allen and Lee, it was the best day ever. For Charlie, it had been a day of new awareness. For the first time, his negative behavior had been treated with the proper response. Allen and Lee had initially been unhappy with Charlie's behavior, but they accepted his apology; they hadn't yelled and screamed at him and told him how worthless he was. Instead, they had asked him to join them on the beach for some fun. And what a day of fun it had been for Charlie.

CHAPTER 18
Charlie

*I*t was the most beautiful day anyone could ask for. The sun was shining, and a cool mist was blowing ever so gently across the beautiful crystal blue ocean. Seagulls were soaring effortlessly across the backdrop of a cloudless sky. Dolphins were jumping high as they soared over the waves and gracefully diving into the water.

Oh yes, this is going to be a great day, I thought as I headed to the water with my new surfboard. Normally I would be swimming in the cool water, enjoying each and every stroke. But not today. I'd worked hard for weeks doing odd jobs for people in Shell Cove, and my new surfboard was my reward. It was emerald-green with sliver seashells scattered across the surface. Each time I surfed, the board sparkled across the waves racing toward the finish line.

Never before had I thought I would love something as much as I did swimming, but that day was a new day in my book of happiness. I'd taken

several lessons on a rented surfboard; the instructor had taken time with me because he sensed the real appreciation I had for the craft. Like swimming, surfing seemed to come naturally to me. I was at ease on the board riding the waves. Even the occasional plunge into the ocean from a wave taken too early or too late was sheer enjoyment.

"Of course, I'll check on Lee and Allen," I had told Mom that morning. "But didn't you tell Lee he could go without supervision to the beach today?"

"You know I did. But I never said I wouldn't have his older brother just stop by to see if he needed anything," she said with a big smile and a wink.

"All right, Mom, no worries, I'll just stop by and say hi, okay?"

"Okay," she replied.

I recalled my conversation with Mom. *I've checked on them once today, but that was earlier this morning. It won't hurt to check on Lee one more time*, I thought as I rode the last wave to shore.

Lee, Allen, and Charlie were enjoying each other's company as if they'd been friends for many years. That was true for Lee and Allen, but Charlie had just joined them for the first time. I joined them again for a brief moment to say hello and make sure they were still okay without letting them know what I was really doing—checking up on them for mom.

"Hey, you guys, got any food left? I'm starving," I asked.

"You're in luck," Lee said as he handed me the last

sandwich and chips. Allen went to the ice chest to get me some Kool-Aid.

"Thanks, guys. This will be great. Glad you made enough to share," I said. I bowed my head and thanked God for the food before devouring it.

Charlie watched in awe as Andrew bowed his head and thanked God for his food. Charlie was wondering about this God that the boys were praying to, for this was all so new for him.

I could see that the boys were doing great without supervision. I felt a little sad and yet joy for my little brother, who was growing up.

The boys asked me to show them how good I could surf and maybe give them a lesson or two. I was more than willing to show off my new skills, but I told them that lessons would have to wait a bit. The boys sadly agreed that for now they'd be happy just watching me surf.

"Come on, guys! The sooner we pack up your things, the sooner I can hit the waves," I said as I put the ice chest in the beach wagon. Lee and Allen began to pack up what was left of the food.

Such togetherness and helping one another was a new and wonderful experience for little Charlie. He joined right in; he was a little timid at first, but that faded quickly.

When everything was loaded and the boys were finally ready to leave that area of the beach, Allen checked out the area for anything they might have left behind. "Must not litter our beautiful beach," he said. Allen was satisfied that they hadn't left any litter and ran to catch up with his friends. Lee pulled the beach wagon and followed me.

"Lee, let me pull the wagon," Charlie said. "After all, you and Allen did all the work preparing for this outing."

Lee handed Charlie the handle of the wagon. "Be my guest."

Charlie smiled at Lee's reply and quickly took the handle. I led them to the area of the beach that was my favorite place to surf. This part of the beach had a small palm tree growing on a large sand dune. The height of the dune would give the boys a better view and the palm tree would provide them with a little shade while they enjoyed the show. Once the boys were settled, I headed back to the beach to the place I had left my surfboard and headed out into the ocean.

The boys were ecstatic as they watched me; I'd mastered my new passion in a short time. They could be seen and heard cheering me on as their arms waved high above their heads to tell me, I was putting on a great show for them. Of course, their cheers would stop briefly as they enjoyed a drink of Kool-Aid and ate the last cookies that remained from the lunch they had packed that morning.

The beach outing was coming to a close. All three boys were tired from their day of sun and fun. Allen and Lee told Charlie that they had to get home before it got too late, they didn't want their mothers worrying about them. Or to think they still needed someone to supervise them. Charlie said he understood, but he was sad to see the day come to an end. He'd had so much fun with Lee and Allen, and he wanted this new feeling of having friends who really cared about him to last.

Charlie knew that when he got home, his parents wouldn't even know he'd been out all day. His mom and dad lived in their own worlds, worlds that had no place for Charlie. He told his new friends that he'd had a great time hanging out with them and that he hoped they could do it again real soon. He made a point of thanking them for the fantastic lunch—"It was the best ever!"

The boys went their separate ways. Allen and Lee left together; their houses were very near. Charlie went in the other direction. He walked briskly at first, but the closer he got to home, the slower his pace became.

"Do you really think those two boys are your friends? They just had pity on you, that's all. The next time you see them, they probably won't even say hello," a voice told Charlie.

Unfortunately, Charlie didn't know the difference between his own thoughts and the thoughts that were placed in his mind by the demons. He had heard their little demonic voices his whole life, and he usually believed every word they told him. When Charlie was born, his parents seemed to be overjoyed by the new addition to their family. However, the everyday task of taking care of him became overwhelming for them, and their own desires became more important than little Charlie.

Once Charlie could feed and dress himself, his parents seemed to all but disappear. Sure, they all lived in the same house, but no one would have known he was their child. Charlie was more like a roommate, and for now his parents did not require him to contribute to the finances. He prepared his own food, washed his own clothes, and for the most part stayed in his room or on the streets just to be out of his parents' way. His parents never hurt Charlie, well at least not with hitting him or some other form of physical abuse. But they sure hurt him emotionally. In their eyes, he was a burden, a mistake, and always in their way.

There were angels that had tried to help Charlie, however their voices became quiet to Charlie for he believed the demonic voices. Because their words matched what his parents told him either verbally or by their actions. And sometimes by their lack of action. But the angels never left Charlie; they hoped that one day, he would hear their voices telling him how much he was loved and that the God who created him didn't think of him as a mistake, but as a beautiful miracle. One day, Charlie would see how wonderful he really was and how much he was truly loved.

Charlie opened the back door of his house slowly; he didn't want it to make its usual creaking noise. He'd had such a great day and didn't want anything to spoil it. He'd heard the voice on his way home telling him bad things about Allen and Lee, but he had not given into it as he normally did. *Nothing's going to take the great memories of my day on the beach with my new friends*, Charlie thought.

He walked softly past his dad, who was asleep on the couch with the TV blaring as usual. His mom was nowhere in sight. He went to his bedroom and closed the door gently behind him. He breathed a sigh of relief. His eyes as always were drawn to the small painting hanging above his bed. The painting of a little boy with curly blond hair sitting in his dad's lap with his mom seated beside them. That was a painting of happier times for Charlie and his parents. His parents' faces shined with love for each other and their little boy.

Charlie had thought about taking the painting down numerous times, but he always hope that the happiness of that day would be restored.

His bedroom was a modest little room, with a twin bed, a bedside table with a lamp, and a chest of drawers. But he didn't mind; his room had become his safe haven for as long as he could remember. His grandparents had given him a small TV, "Just for you," they had said. He'd been overjoyed with the gift; it meant he didn't have to join his parents in the living room to watch TV.

Charlie's room was on the other side of the house from his parents' bedroom and the other living areas. His room even had a small bathroom right next to it. No one really ever came to that side of the house, well except for Charlie.

Charlie opened his bedroom door gently and walked slowly and quietly down the narrow, dark hallway that led to the kitchen. He didn't want to turn the lights on for fear of waking his dad. The sandwiches and cookies he had eaten with Lee and Allen was the only meal he'd had all day, and his growling stomach told him it was time to eat. Charlie and his mom arrived in the kitchen within seconds of one another.

"Charlie, where have you been all day?"

"Hanging out with my friends on the beach."

He was so happy to have boys he could call his friends. A big grin came across his face and a twinkle could be seen in his eyes.

"What friends? I've never seen you with any friends before," his mom said in a most hateful way. "And what's that grin on your face for? You find something funny?"

"No, mom, I just had a nice time on the beach, that's all. What's for supper?" he asked sheepishly.

"Believe it or not, I cooked us a nice roast with all the trimmings," she said in a cheery voice, one that Charlie didn't recognize. "I put a plate for you in the fridge. Clean up when you're finished," she said as she walked out of the kitchen.

Charlie couldn't believe it when he opened the door to the refrigerator—there sat a plate of roast beef with potatoes and carrots. He microwaved the food and then sat down for his meal. He had just placed a forkful of tender roast beef into his mouth when Lee's words came back to him—"We always give God thanks before we eat." He put his fork down. There wasn't anyone to hold hands with, so he put his small hands together, bowed his head, and said his first prayer: "God, I'm not sure who you are or where you live, but my new friends, Lee and Allen, say a prayer to you before they eat. I've never said a prayer before, but here goes! Thank you, God, for my food, and thank you for my new friends, amen!"

He ate everything on his plate, washed the dishes, and returned to his room. He watched some TV and realized he was very tired from the day's sun and fun. He brushed his teeth, put on his PJs, and jumped into bed. Then he immediately jumped out of bed and kneeled on the small tattered rug bedside his bed. He bowed his head and folded his hands. "God? I'm not sure if this is correct, or not, but I just wanted to say thank You for the great day. So, God, thank You and goodnight."

He jumped back into bed and was soon fast asleep. His dreams were most pleasant, they were filled with happy thoughts of the day's events.

CHAPTER 19
The Headstones

"Paige, do you have plans to meet your friends today?" her mom asked.

Paige and her mom were having lunch at the Star Café as they did when it was their girls' day out. They had an early morning at the hair salon followed by manicures and pedicures.

"No, Mom. I thought this was our day," Paige replied.

"I'm sorry, Paige but I promised to help with the church newcomers' welcome dinner later today. When I agreed to help, our girls' day out was scheduled for next Saturday, remember?"

"That's right," Paige said with a little expression of excitement on her face that her mom didn't understand. "I forgot that I changed the day because of a school project. It's okay, Mom. You go help the church. I'm sure I can find something else to do."

Again, Paige's mom noticed she seemed excited about not spending the rest of the day with her.

"Paige, you seem glad I have to cancel the rest of our day."

Her mom's face showed sadness and hurt by Paige's seeming excitement at their girls' day out being cut short.

Paige quickly replied, "Mom, I love our girls' day out. I was just thinking that if you and I can't go to the movies, I'd take a walk through the old cemetery."

"The old cemetery?" her mom asked a little intensely. For a brief moment, all eyes in the small café turned to them. "Why on earth would you be going to the old cemetery?"

Paige wasn't sure what, if any of this new knowledge she had acquired should be shared with her mom. She had never kept secrets from her parents before. Then Amethyst appeared. Paige knew that meant it wasn't time to share anything with her mom.

"Mom, I just find the old headstones interesting to read. I'm kind of doing a research on the town's history."

Her mom gave her a big smile of approval; she was delighted that her daughter was doing research even if it was in the old cemetery. "Paige, that's an excellent idea. What better way to get to know a towns' history then finding out about its first residents."

"Mom, before we leave, I was wondering if I can ask you a question?"

"Of course, Paige you can ask me anything."

"Do you believe in angels? Have you ever seen one?"

"Of course, I believe in angels. The Bible tells us about them. I'm not sure I've ever seen one, but maybe when I was a child. People say that children can see angels but as we grow up, we lose that gift."

"Why do you call it a gift?"

"I think that if you're allowed to see angels, God or Jesus must have given you the ability to do so, and to me that would be a great gift!"

Paige was now looking at her mom with much curiosity. She was overjoyed to hear that her mom believed in angels, but she wanted to know if her mom believed in demons as well. Paige was thrilled to have learned that not only did angels exist but also that they appeared to and talked with people. She wasn't thrilled at all to have learned demons were real as well.

"So, does that mean you also believe in demons?"

Paige's mom took a few seconds before she answered her daughter's question. Hyson did believe in demons but didn't want to frighten her daughter unnecessarily. "Paige, these are very unusual questions coming from you. They would be normal coming from Michael, yes, but not you."

"Mom, when I'm at the old cemetery, things like that just pop into my head."

"Seems to me you've watched way too many horror movies," her mom said with a nervous laugh.

"So that's your answer? Too many horror movies? Really, Mom? I thought I'd at least get a Webster's dictionary answer from an intelligent woman," Paige said as she looked over the top of her glasses. She was like a reporter interviewing a professor and didn't believe the answer she'd just received.

"I'm sorry, Ms. Paige, but this interview is over," Hyson said.

The two tried to contain their laughter, but it was wasted effort. The other people in the café stared just long enough to cause Hyson and Paige to again break out into delightful laughter. They decided it was time to leave, they again shared smiles and left the café. Paige gave her mom a big hug and kiss on her cheek.

"What was that for?"

"I just love you, Mom, that's all." Then they parted ways.

On the way to the old cemetery, Amethyst joined Paige.

"Paige, your mom loves you very much!"

"Yes, I know, but how did you know that?" Paige asked.

"I can see it in her eyes each time she looks at you."

Amethyst knew that Hyson believed in angels and demons as well, but she didn't think the information was for her to share with Paige. *If Hyson wants her daughter to know about demons, she'll tell her,* Amethyst thought.

Paige opened the gate to the old cemetery, which gave out its usual squeaky invitation. "I've decided to write down what's on the headstones that speak to me," Paige said, thinking she was still talking to Amethyst, but Amethyst was nowhere to be found. *That's strange,* Paige thought. *Oh well, on with the task at hand.*

Walking slowing through the old cemetery, Paige took

notice of everything. The clouds were a bluish gray and appeared to be moving quickly across the sky as if in a race to the finish line. The mossy tree branches were hanging low and slowly swaying in the misty breeze; they seemed to be saying, *Come on in! We've been waiting for you.* Paige laughed softly to herself. *Too many horror movies will do that to you.*

She passed the first few headstones; nothing happened. *Well this is a big waste of time. Maybe I imaged that the words lit up? How crazy is that when you think about it?* She continued walking slowly through the old cemetery, looking quickly here and there as if her actions would make something happen. Finally, she sat on a bench under a big palm tree. *Maybe they glow only at night.* She watched birds building a nest in a nearby tree. She noticed that the birds were going to the headstones and taking old flowers and leaves from vases people had left for their loved ones. That's when she noticed a word glowing as if had been waiting for her attention.

Henry Mitchell
Born October 20, 1703—Eternal Life November 12, 1775
Beloved Husband and Father
Your song has ended much too soon!
Your new song of Praise has just begun
Of eternal life with everlasting love.

Hyson Mitchell
Born February 16, 1702—Eternal Life March 4, 1769
Dearly Beloved Wife and Mother
Our hearts will forever miss you, and the treasure that you
were.
You will always be remembered as a jewel from above.

Captain Herbert Mize
Born June 7, 1710—Eternal Life November 21, 1771
Dearly Beloved Husband, Dad, and Sea Captain
Behold my friends as you proceed by,
As I am now, so shall you be.
Please give thyself to Jesus and follow me.

Henrietta Mize
Born July 5, 1726—Eternal Life September 14, 1807
Devoted Wife and Mother
She took in all the beauty this world had to offer,
And arranged it in beautiful bouquets to show us God's
love.
Always loving, Always loved.

Immanuel Garza

Born May 18, 1701—Eternal Life January 15, 1768

Husband and Father, loved by all

Your journey on this new adventure

will be even happier than your time spent with us.

Martha Garza

Born May 18, 1708—Eternal Life March 12, 1770

Devoted Wife and Mother

Do not cry for her now,

Just smile a smile of no regrets.

She was a precious diamond in this world,

And that diamond sparkles yet!

Nathaniel George

Born February 10, 1708—Eternal Life December 20, 1772

Beloved Husband and Father

Helping others was a gift he had that compared to no other!

The generosity of his heart gave him wealth beyond compare.

Sarah Moss

Born October 20, 1712—Eternal Life August 10, 1771

Beloved Wife and Mother

We miss you very much and love you dearly.

Our hearts are at peace knowing God is taking care of you.

Rebecca Judge
Born November 24, 1710—Eternal Life March 4, 1775
Beloved Wife and Mother
She was too well loved to ever be forgotten!
Our hearts are full of peace knowing she has victory in Jesus.

Jonathan Judge
Born March 19, 1708—Eternal Life September 6, 1774
Dearly Beloved Pastor, Husband, and Father
Death is only the path that leads to heaven.
It holds the key that opens the gate to eternal life.

Jeannette Heinrich
Born August 1, 1703—Eternal Life April 9, 1756
Wonderful Wife and Mother
To the world, you may have been just a woman.
But for all of us, you made our world complete.
This world will be a dimmer place without the bright light of love you gave us.

Robert Heinrich
Born January 19, 1705—Eternal Life April 21, 1776
Beloved Husband and Father
Life is a voyage that takes us to our eternal home,
An eternal home of love and sunshine without end.

CHAPTER 20
The Others

I knew in my heart that each and every battle would be something the gang had never dreamed of, much less faced. I also knew I had prepared the gang as instructed by God. Brian had made sure that I hadn't missed anything during my lessons. Brian knew the gang was well prepared for what lay ahead.

"If we run into the others, which we now know are demons, don't be afraid or back down. Remember what you have learned over the past few months. Nothing or no one can harm us! We are strong in the Lord and in the power of His might!" I told the gang.

The gang listened intently to me, I had become their true leader; they all had great respect for me. Once I'd finished talking, the only one with a question was Allen.

"Andrew? "Allen said as he raised his hand to get my attention.

"Yes, Allen." I replied

"Can we play on the beach now?" Allen asked.

I made a jester with my hands like a teacher dismissing a class. With this a loud joyful laughter was made by all. They raced off to our favorite spot on the beach. I didn't join them right away; I'd learned to discern when the spirit world around me was no longer friendly. I knew the demons were there, but no longer did fear embrace me when I thought about this new foe.

There was an air of uncertainty that loomed over us as we made our way to our special spot on the beach. We were waiting for our first encounter with the demons. But as soon as we hit the beach the loom of uncertainty turned into a ray of sunshine dissipating our uncertainty into the safe cool misty breeze blowing gently in from the ocean.

The day turned into just another great day at the beach. The sand was shining, glistening like jewels twirling in the waves, while sunrays dance on the water. Lee and Allen were busy building yet another great sandcastle. I was swimming in the ocean or riding the waves. Paige and Sally were laying on their beach towels, their bodies covered in suntan lotion. Michael and his crew were exploring a newfound island his ship has landed on.

"Look for fresh fruit and water to restock before we shove off on our next adventure," he shouted as if there really were a crew to shout to.

In the unseen world, which humans cannot see with their human eyes, there was much activity. The ghoulish creatures with hollow, sunken eyes continued to watch the gang. They had always been there plotting and planning their evil deeds. Not even the weak demons gave the gang a second thought. Until recently. The demons felt an unwelcome change in their world. One they had never felt before. Sure, there had been times when they'd gotten too close to the church or near certain houses in the town that they felt a slight undertow of this overwhelming light. But it had never been that strong before, and never on the beach.

It was Saturday, and we all could stay out later than on school nights. No one wanted to leave the beach.

"Maybe we can get our parents to cook out here tonight," Lee said.

"Let's go see," Allen said.

They ran to their houses as if they would receive trophies at the finish line.

Allen's mom was in the kitchen making dinner, and to his surprise, it was hotdogs for a picnic on the beach. When Lee arrived at his house, he saw that his mom was doing the same thing. To the gang's surprise, their moms had gotten together earlier that day to arrange for an outdoor dinner of hotdogs, chips, lemonade, and cake.

Lee and Allen ran back to the beach even faster than they had run home. Running was never a problem for the two of them; it was stopping that presented some difficulties. Of course, their brakes failed, and they tumbled over Paige and Sally and all their suntan lotion. That sent the girls running to the ocean to get the sand off and yelling at Lee and Allen all the way to the water.

"What do you mean your brakes failed? You don't have brakes!" Sally shouted.

That made Allen, Lee, and Michael break out into their famous belly laughs, which made the girls even madder.

However, no one was mad when their moms appeared at the picnic area of the beach with baskets full of goodies.

When dinner was over, the parents headed home giving them until sunset to play at the beach. The gang gathered their towels and headed to their special place. That would be the first time Sally had been allowed into their sanctuary.

The sky is so beautiful this time of day, Sally thought as she followed Paige around the corner and into the cave.

Sally stopped in her tracks. "This is unbelievable! She said with all the excitement she could summon. "I've never seen such a beautiful waterfall, and the pool below—oh my!"

"You sound just like me the first time Andrew showed us this place," Paige said.

"I found this place when I was swimming and got caught in an undertow," I said. "You know how the experts tell us to just go with it, not fight it. Well that's what I did, and it brought me here." I was waving my arms as if I were a tour guide wanting everyone to see the many wonders awaiting them.

"Pretty cool, huh?" Michael said.

Cool is an understatement Sally thought but did not say because she thought it might hurt Michael's feelings. She just smiled in agreement with him.

We all felt at peace there even after all we had been told about the demons. Paige began singing a song, the melody was very catchy, but the others didn't know the words. Paige was always singing songs—pop, country, rock 'n' roll, but not church songs.

This is definitely a church song, I thought as I listened to the words. Soon, everyone joined in as if we had all practiced the song before. We swayed, almost dancing to the melody with arms stretched to the sky in effortless praise to God. When we finished singing, everyone looked at each other with an overwhelming feeling of peace and joy.

"It's time we head out of here," I said. "The sun's starting to set. There will be just enough light for us to get home."

Everyone left the cave and headed home.

"Stop that, Michael! That's not funny!" Lee said as he wiped sand off his pants.

"What are you talking about?" Michael asked.

"You know! You pushed me down."

"Hey! Who just hit me with something?" Allen shouted.

We all stopped dead in our tracks and looked at each other. Michael couldn't have pushed Lee into the sand because he had been several feet in front of Lee. And there wasn't anyone behind Allen to throw anything at him.

"This is all very strange!" Sally said.

That's when all hell broke loose. The demons we'd heard so much about from the guardian angels just appeared. And just as the angels had warned us, these demons weren't friendly at all. They began grabbing us by our arms with their blackish hands or claws or whatever they were. Their eyes were dark-black with fiery-red speckles. When they spoke, they sounded kind and sweet at first, but that quickly turned into a deep, growling, undesirable sound. We realized that the demons meant us harm.

I quickly went into action. "Allen! Lee! All of you come over here. Let's put our backs against each other!"

Now back to back, the whole gang could see all around us. One of the bigger demons came right up to me. The closer he got, the bigger he appeared.

"So, you think you and your gang are ready to take us on?" Raef spew out at me. All the other demons seemed to gather a little courage from that move. They too began to appear bigger and meaner as they came closer and closer to us.

We were quickly surrounded! And from the look of things, we realized we were more than outnumbered by the demons. The demons had claws, sharp teeth, and fire; they were soldiers in a demonic army. *We were just a group of kids—no weapons and not soldiers in any army. At least that was how the demons saw us,* I thought. But that was the demons' first mistake. I felt no fear as I faced this demonic army. I said just one word, and the demons fled leaving dark, smoky, foul-smelling trails behind them.

That's when the words on the headstones Paige had written down all made sense to her: "Praise Proceeds Victory."

Michael asked, "What just happened?" as if he couldn't believe what he had just seen.

Everyone started firing questions at me, so I shouted, "Back to the cave!" The gang ran as fast as they could. I brought up the rear; I didn't want anyone left out there alone.

Once we were all inside, I said, "You know, when we first met the guardian angels, it was hard for any of us to believe what we were seeing and hearing. And what we were told about the demons was even more difficult to believe. Tonight, we faced the demons, and I know it was very frightening for all of us. But tonight, proved that what we've read and been taught is all true! The demons may try to attack us again. The next time, they might attack us individually. We have more power when we're together. Just remember that the guardian angels are always with us."

The gang began singing as if what had happened to us had never taken place. That's when "the peace that surpasses all understanding" floated down from the sky and covered us all like a feathery blanket.

When we finished singing, we headed home, and that time, we made it home safely.

The unseen world wasn't happy. Not that demons were ever happy as humans could be. Their world was filled with hate, contempt, and despair. The madder the demons got, the hotter their world became.

"This will not do," Raef said. He, the ugliest demon of them all, was pacing in front of the lesser demons. "I've been sent here to unravel this little piece of heaven as the humans call it. Before I'm done, the humans will call this place hell!"

Rail, a demon of equal rank, walked straight up to Raef clapping his fiery red hands. The other demons tried to take cover, for it wasn't the first encounter between these two demons, and their encounters never ended well. Usually, one or two lesser demons would be sent straight back to hell during their outburst.

"That's big talk coming from a demon who just lost his first battle with a gang of children," Rail said.

"Watch your mouth, Rail, or you'll be taking a fast ride straight to hell with several of your buddies," shouted Raef with fire and smoke coming out of his mouth with each syllable.

That caused the other demons to run; they knew what Raef was threatening, and they knew he could make it happen.

"The master has sent me here to assist you with your mission," Rail continued as if he hadn't heard what Raef had said.

"What are you talking about? This is my mission and mine alone!" replied Raef. "I do not want or need your help!"

"What you want, Raef, is no concern of mine," Rail replied. "The master just witnessed your little encounter with the gang, as they like to call themselves, and let me just say he wasn't pleased! The next thing I knew, I was standing in front of him receiving my orders. And here I am!"

Once the gang were all home and safely tucked in bed, each one of them began to think back on the night's events. Not one of them felt fear when they remembered what had taken place. Their thoughts were all on the one word that Andrew had said that sent the demons fleeing. That one word was *Jesus*!

This is not the end of their story—only a small portion of it. Many adventures still lay ahead for the gang who live in Shell Cove on Starfish Island.

PAIGE'S SONG

Praise the Lord!
Sing unto Him a new song.

Rejoice in the Lord!
For His word is right.

Praise the Lord!
Let us exalt His name together.

Praise the Lord!
Morning, noon and night.

Repeat

MEET THE GANG

Meet The Gang

Allen

Andrew

Michael

Paige

Lee

MEET THE ANGELS

THE DEMONS

Printed and bound by PG in the USA

USA20198GIL